easy
stir-fry

easy
stir-fry

100 fuss-free recipes for everyday cooking

MARKS &
SPENCER

Marks and Spencer p.l.c.
PO Box 3339
Chester CH99 9QS

shop online
www.marksandspencer.com

ISBN: 978-1-84960-752-0

Printed in China

Introduction by Linda Doeser
New recipes by Sandra Baddeley
Cover photography by Clive Streeter
Additional photography by Mike Cooper
Cover food styling by Teresa Goldfinch
Additional food styling by Sumi Glass

The views expressed in this book are those of the author but they
are general views only and readers are urged to consult a relevant
and qualified specialist for individual advice in particular situations.
Marks and Spencer p.l.c. and Exclusive Editions Limited hereby
exclude all liability to the extent permitted by law for any errors
or omissions in this book and for any loss, damage or expense
(whether direct or indirect) suffered by a third party relying on any
information contained in this book.

Notes for the Reader
This book uses both metric and imperial measurements. Follow
the same units of measurement throughout; do not mix metric and
imperial. All spoon measurements are level: teaspoons are assumed
to be 5 ml, and tablespoons are assumed to be 15 ml. Unless
otherwise stated, milk is assumed to be full fat, eggs and individual
vegetables are medium, and pepper is freshly ground black pepper.

The times given are an approximate guide only. Preparation times
differ according to the techniques used by different people and
the cooking times may also vary from those given. Optional
ingredients, variations or serving suggestions have not been
included in the calculations.

Recipes using raw or very lightly cooked eggs should be avoided
by infants, the elderly, pregnant women, convalescents and anyone
suffering from an illness. Pregnant and breastfeeding women are
advised to avoid eating peanuts and peanut products. Sufferers
from nut allergies should be aware that some of the ready-made
ingredients used in the recipes in this book may contain nuts.
Always check the packaging before use.

For front cover recipe, please see page 22

Contents

Introduction

Invented as a way of cooking food in a country where fuel was scarce, stir-frying must be one of China's most successful exports. Although domestic fuel is becoming increasingly expensive in the West, it is still easily available; what we are all short of is time. Although preparing ingredients for stir-frying may take a little while, cooking them usually takes a matter of minutes.

While there is a wealth of different recipes using a wide range of ingredients, the basic technique of stir-frying is the same. For professional results, invest in a good-quality wok – a bowl-shaped pan with sloping sides that will allow the heat to spread evenly and rapidly.

Heat the empty wok over a high heat for a few minutes, then add the oil and swirl it around the inside of the wok to coat the base and halfway up the sides.

When the oil is hot, but not smoking, the ingredients are added in the order given in the recipe. Aromatics, such as ginger, garlic and spring onions, are added first and it is a good idea to lower the heat slightly. Stir and toss them in the oil for only a few seconds.

Ingredients that require longer cooking – meat, poultry and dense vegetables such as carrots – are added next and, finally, faster-cooking ingredients – mangetouts, spinach, beansprouts and herbs – towards the end of the cooking time. Increase the heat again once the main ingredients have been added and keep tossing and turning them from the centre of the wok to the outside.

The advantages of this 'fast food' go way beyond simply saving on cooking time. Cooking the ingredients so quickly helps to retain their flavour, colour and texture, as well as their nutritional content. Very little oil is required so stir-fried dishes are relatively low in fat and this also helps to retain the nutritional content.

China is such a vast country it is hardly surprising that recipes vary widely from one region to another – light, subtle and featuring seafood in the south, hotly spiced and strongly flavoured in the west, for example.

However, the variety of stir-fried dishes is even more extensive as the technique is also widely used throughout South-east Asia, in Japan and on the Indian sub-continent where the wok has been replaced by the similar karahi.

Top Tips for Success

• When using a new wok, scrub off the protective layer of oil and season it first according to the manufacturer's instructions. Do not scrub again once it has been seasoned; after use simply wash it in hot water (without detergent) and dry thoroughly. If rust appears, scour it off and season the wok again.

• Read all the way through the recipe before you start and assemble all the ingredients and equipment you will require. Once you start stir-frying, it will be so rapid that there is no time for poking about in a cupboard looking for soy sauce or a lemon squeezer.

• Chinese cooks use a cleaver for cutting and slicing, even when handling small delicate ingredients, such as prawns. If you don't feel confident using a cleaver, you can use a cook's knife with a heavy blade and a well-balanced handle. Whichever you choose, sharpen it regularly. A sharp knife is easier and safer to use than a blunt one which requires more pressure and can easily slip. Store in a knife block or on a magnetic rack, not in a drawer where the blade may become chipped and/or blunted.

• Successful stir-frying depends on the ingredients cooking as quickly as possible, yet still absorbing flavours and aromas. Therefore, you must cut them into small pieces of uniform size, preferably with as many cut surfaces as possible that can be exposed to the heat. Cut vegetables, such as carrots and spring onions, diagonally by holding the knife at a slant. Cut large vegetables, such as courgettes and aubergines, with a roll cut. To do this, start with a diagonal cut at one end of the vegetable, then turn it through 180° and make another diagonal cut. Continue in this way until the whole vegetable has been cut into even-sized pieces. Shred leafy greens, such as Chinese cabbage, spinach and lettuce, and separate cauliflower and broccoli into small florets.

• If meat is to be cut into paper-thin slices, put it into the freezer for 1 hour first. This makes it much easier to cut thinly. Always cut beef across the grain to prevent it from becoming tough. You can cut chicken, lamb and pork across or along the grain.

• The type of oil used for stir-frying varies, but nut, corn or sunflower oils are most suitable.

• Never leave the wok unattended over the heat. If an emergency means that you must leave the kitchen, remove the wok from the heat and turn off the heat.

Mouth-watering Meat

beef chop suey

SERVES 4

450 g/1 lb ribeye or sirloin
steak, finely sliced

1 head of broccoli, cut into
small florets

2 tbsp vegetable or
groundnut oil

1 onion, finely sliced

2 celery stalks, finely
sliced diagonally

225 g/8 oz mangetout,
sliced in half lengthways

55 g/2 oz fresh or canned
bamboo shoots, rinsed
and julienned (if using
fresh shoots, boil in
water first for
30 minutes)

8 water chestnuts,
finely sliced

225 g/8 oz mushrooms,
finely sliced

1 tbsp oyster sauce

1 tsp salt

cooked rice, to serve

marinade

1 tbsp Shaoxing rice wine

pinch of white pepper

pinch of salt

1 tbsp light soy sauce

½ tsp sesame oil

1 Combine all the marinade ingredients in a bowl and
marinate the beef for at least 20 minutes. Blanch the
broccoli in a large pan of boiling water for 30 seconds. Drain
and set aside.

2 In a preheated wok, heat 1 tablespoon of the oil and
stir-fry the beef until the colour has changed. Remove
and set aside. Wipe the wok clean.

3 In the clean wok, heat the remaining oil and stir-fry the
onion for 1 minute. Add the celery and broccoli and cook
for 2 minutes. Add the mangetout, bamboo shoots, chestnuts
and mushrooms and cook for 1 minute. Add the beef, then
season with the oyster sauce and salt and serve with freshly
cooked rice.

beef with mixed mushrooms

SERVES 2–3

1½ tbsp Szechuan peppercorns

½ tsp salt

350 g/12 oz sirloin or rump steak

200 g/7 oz mixed small mushrooms, such as cremini, enoki and buna shimeji

½ tbsp cornflour

125 ml/4 fl oz beef stock

2 tsp Chinese rice wine or dry sherry

4 tsp soy sauce

3 tbsp groundnut oil

1 shallot, finely chopped

1 tsp finely chopped fresh ginger

1 large garlic clove, thinly sliced

3 tbsp chopped fresh coriander, to garnish

1 Grind the Szechuan peppercorns with the salt, using a mortar and pestle. Sprinkle over both sides of the meat, pressing in well. Slice the meat diagonally across the grain into thin bite-sized pieces and set aside.

2 Rinse the mushrooms and dry with kitchen paper. If using clumping mushrooms, such as enoki and buna shimeji, slice off the root and separate the clump. Slice cremini mushrooms in half.

3 Mix the cornflour to a paste with 2 tablespoons of the stock. Add the rice wine and soy sauce, mixing well. Heat a wok over a medium–high heat, then add 1 tablespoon of the oil. Fry the shallot and ginger for 1 minute. Add the garlic and fry for a few seconds, then add the mushrooms and 2 tablespoons of the stock.

4 Stir-fry for 4 minutes. Add the cornflour mixture and the remaining stock. Bring to the boil, stirring, then reduce the heat and simmer for 2 minutes. Transfer to a warmed serving dish.

5 Clean the wok and heat over a high heat. Add the remaining oil. Add the beef and stir-fry for 3 minutes. Add to the mushroom mixture and garnish with the coriander. Serve immediately.

hot sesame beef

SERVES 4

**500 g/1 lb 2 oz beef fillet,
cut into thin strips**

1½ tbsp sesame seeds

125 ml/4 fl oz beef stock

2 tbsp soy sauce

2 tbsp grated fresh ginger

**2 garlic cloves, finely
chopped**

1 tsp cornflour

½ tsp chilli flakes

3 tbsp sesame oil

**1 large head of broccoli,
cut into florets**

**1 yellow pepper, thinly
sliced**

**1 red chilli, deseeded and
finely sliced**

1 tbsp chilli oil, to taste

**1 tbsp chopped fresh
coriander, to garnish**

1 Mix the beef strips with 1 tablespoon of the sesame seeds in a small bowl. In a separate bowl, whisk together the beef stock, soy sauce, ginger, garlic, cornflour and chilli flakes.

2 Heat 1 tablespoon of the sesame oil in a large preheated wok or frying pan. Stir-fry the beef strips for 2–3 minutes. Remove and set aside.

3 Discard any remaining oil in the pan, then wipe with kitchen paper to remove any stray sesame seeds. Heat the remaining oil, add the broccoli, pepper, chilli and chilli oil and stir-fry for 2–3 minutes. Stir in the beef stock mixture, cover and simmer for 2 minutes.

4 Return the beef to the wok and simmer until the juices thicken, stirring occasionally. Cook for another 1–2 minutes.

5 Sprinkle with the remaining sesame seeds. Garnish with fresh coriander.

chilli beef
stir-fry salad

SERVES 4

**450 g/1 lb rump steak,
cut into thin strips**

1 ripe avocado

2 tbsp sunflower oil

**425 g/15 oz canned red
kidney beans, drained**

**175 g/6 oz cherry tomatoes,
halved**

1 large packet tortilla chips

iceberg lettuce, shredded

**chopped fresh coriander,
to garnish**

marinade

2 garlic cloves, crushed

1 tsp chilli powder

½ tsp salt

1 tsp ground coriander

1 For the marinade, place the garlic, chilli powder, salt and ground coriander in a large bowl and stir until well mixed.

2 Add the strips of beef to the marinade and toss thoroughly to coat all over.

3 Using a sharp knife, peel the avocado. Slice the avocado lengthways in half and remove and discard the stone, then slice crossways to form small dice.

4 Heat the oil in a large preheated wok. Add the beef and stir-fry for 5 minutes, tossing frequently. Add the kidney beans, tomatoes and avocado and cook for 2 minutes.

5 Arrange the tortilla chips and iceberg lettuce around the edge of a serving plate and spoon the beef into the centre. Alternatively, serve the tortilla chips and lettuce separately. Garnish with fresh coriander and serve immediately.

beef with broccoli & ginger

SERVES 4–6

350 g/12 oz fillet steak, cut into thin strips

175 g/6 oz broccoli florets

2 tbsp vegetable or groundnut oil

1 garlic clove, finely chopped

1 tsp finely chopped fresh ginger

1 small onion, finely sliced

1 tsp salt

1 tsp light soy sauce

marinade

1 tbsp light soy sauce

1 tsp sesame oil

1 tsp Shaoxing rice wine

1 tsp sugar

pinch of white pepper

1 Combine the marinade ingredients in a bowl, then mix in the beef. Cover and leave to stand for 1 hour, basting occasionally. Blanch the broccoli in a large pan of boiling water for 30 seconds. Drain and set aside.

2 In a preheated wok, heat 1 tablespoon of the oil and stir-fry the garlic, ginger and onion for 1 minute. Add the broccoli and stir-fry for a further minute. Remove from the wok and set aside. Wipe the wok clean.

3 Preheat the clean wok, heat the remaining oil and stir-fry the beef until the colour has changed. Return the broccoli mixture to the wok with the salt and light soy sauce and stir until cooked through. Serve immediately.

marinated beef with vegetables

SERVES 4–6

500 g/1 lb 2 oz rump steak, cut into thin strips

3 tbsp sesame oil

½ tbsp cornflour

½ tbsp soy sauce

1 head of broccoli, cut into florets

2 carrots, cut into thin strips

115 g/4 oz mangetout

125 ml/4 fl oz beef stock

250 g/9 oz baby spinach, shredded

cooked white rice or noodles, to serve

marinade

1 tbsp dry sherry

½ tbsp soy sauce

½ tbsp cornflour

½ tsp caster sugar

2 garlic cloves, finely chopped

1 tbsp sesame oil

1 To make the marinade, mix the sherry, soy sauce, cornflour, sugar, garlic and sesame oil in a bowl. Add the beef to the mixture, cover with clingfilm and set aside to marinate for 30 minutes.

2 Heat 1 tablespoon of the oil in a preheated wok or frying pan. Stir-fry the beef with its marinade for 2 minutes until medium-rare. Discard the marinade. Remove the beef from the pan and set aside.

3 Combine the cornflour and soy sauce in a bowl and set aside. Pour the remaining 2 tablespoons of sesame oil into the pan, add the broccoli, carrots and mangetout and stir-fry for 2 minutes.

4 Add the stock, cover the pan and steam for 1 minute. Stir in the spinach, beef and the cornflour mixture. Cook until the juices boil and thicken.

5 Serve over freshly cooked white rice or noodles.

soy & sesame beef

SERVES 4

2 tbsp sesame seeds

2 tbsp vegetable oil

**450 g/1 lb beef fillet, thinly
sliced**

**1 green pepper, thinly
sliced**

4 garlic cloves, crushed

2 tbsp dry sherry

4 tbsp soy sauce

6 spring onions, sliced

cooked noodles, to serve

1 Heat a large wok or frying pan until it is very hot.

2 Add the sesame seeds to the wok and dry-fry, stirring, for 1–2 minutes or until they just begin to brown. Take the wok off the heat, remove the sesame seeds and set them aside until required.

3 Heat the vegetable oil in the wok. Add the beef and stir-fry for 2–3 minutes or until sealed on all sides. Then add the sliced pepper and crushed garlic to the wok and continue stir-frying for 2 minutes.

4 Add the dry sherry and soy sauce to the wok, together with the spring onions. Allow the mixture to bubble, stirring occasionally, for about 1 minute, but do not let the mixture burn.

5 Transfer the garlic beef stir-fry to warmed serving bowls and scatter with the dry-fried sesame seeds. Serve immediately with freshly cooked noodles.

thai beef

SERVES 4

2 tbsp vegetable or groundnut oil

2 tbsp Thai green curry paste

2 x 175-g/6-oz sirloin steaks, thinly sliced

2 onions, sliced

6 spring onions, chopped

2 shallots, finely chopped

225 g/8 oz head of broccoli, cut into florets

400 ml/14 fl oz coconut milk

3 kaffir lime leaves, roughly chopped

4 tbsp chopped fresh coriander

handful of Thai basil leaves

1 Heat the oil in a preheated wok and stir-fry the curry paste for 1–2 minutes. Add the beef, in batches if necessary, and stir-fry until starting to brown.

2 Add the onions, spring onions and shallots, and stir-fry for 2–3 minutes. Add the broccoli and stir-fry for 2–3 minutes. Pour in the coconut milk, add the lime leaves and bring to the boil.

3 Simmer gently for 8–10 minutes, until the meat is tender. Stir in the coriander and basil and serve immediately.

ginger beef with yellow peppers

SERVES 4

500 g/1 lb 2 oz beef fillet, cut into 2.5-cm/1-inch cubes

2 tsp groundnut oil

2 garlic cloves, crushed

2 tbsp grated fresh ginger

pinch of chilli flakes

2 yellow peppers, thinly sliced

125 g/4½ oz baby sweetcorn

175 g/6 oz mangetout

cooked noodles drizzled with sesame oil, to serve

marinade

2 tbsp soy sauce

2 tsp groundnut oil

1½ tsp caster sugar

1 tsp cornflour

1 To make the marinade, mix the soy sauce, groundnut oil, sugar and cornflour in a bowl. Stir in the beef, then cover with clingfilm and set aside to marinate for 30 minutes.

2 Heat the groundnut oil in a preheated wok or frying pan over a medium heat. Add the garlic, ginger and chilli flakes and cook for 30 seconds. Stir in the yellow peppers and baby sweetcorn, and stir-fry for 2 minutes. Add the mangetout and cook for another minute. Remove the vegetables and set aside.

3 Put the beef and marinade into the wok and stir-fry for 3–4 minutes or until cooked to taste. Return the vegetables to the wok, mix well and cook until all the ingredients are heated through.

4 Remove from the heat and serve over the freshly cooked noodles.

hot & spicy beef with pine nuts

SERVES 4

450 g/1 lb rump steak, cut into thin strips

55 g/2 oz pine nuts

juice of 1 lime

1 tbsp soy sauce

2 tbsp white wine vinegar

1 tsp cornflour

2 tbsp groundnut oil

3 tsp grated fresh ginger

2 red, hot chillies, finely chopped

4 small baby leeks, halved

2 carrots, thinly sliced

100 g/3½ oz fine tip asparagus

3 shallots, thinly sliced

cooked noodles, to serve

marinade

2 tbsp soy sauce

1 tbsp cornflour

1 tbsp water

1 To make the marinade, mix the soy sauce with the cornflour and water in a medium bowl. Add the beef and stir until the meat is well coated. Cover the bowl with clingfilm and chill in the refrigerator for 1 hour. Spread the pine nuts on a baking sheet and toast under the grill until lightly browned. Remove from under the heat and set aside to cool.

2 Mix the lime juice, soy sauce, vinegar, cornflour and 1 tablespoon of the groundnut oil in a small bowl and set aside. Heat the remaining groundnut oil in a large preheated wok or frying pan. Stir-fry the ginger, chillies and leeks for 2 minutes. Add the beef and the marinade and stir-fry for a further minute.

3 Stir in the carrots, asparagus and shallots and fry for several minutes or until the beef is cooked through. Add the lime mixture, reduce the heat and simmer until the liquid thickens. Remove from the heat, sprinkle with the pine nuts and serve with freshly cooked noodles.

thai marinated beef with celery

SERVES 4

500 g/1 lb 2 oz beef fillet, cut into thin strips

250 ml/9 fl oz vegetable oil

3 celery stalks, cut into 2.5-cm/1-inch thin strips

1 red pepper, cut into thin strips

1 red chilli, deseeded and finely sliced

Thai fish sauce, to serve

lime quarters, to serve

marinade

1 tsp salt

2 tbsp Thai fish sauce

1 To make the marinade, mix the salt and fish sauce in a large bowl. Add the beef and toss to coat. Cover with clingfilm and put in the refrigerator for 1 hour to marinate.

2 Heat 225 ml/8 fl oz of the oil in a preheated wok and stir-fry the beef over a medium heat for 2–3 minutes until crispy. Remove the wok from the heat and, using a slotted spoon, lift out the meat and drain it on kitchen paper. Discard all but 2 tablespoons of the oil.

3 Heat the remaining oil in the wok and stir-fry the celery, red pepper and chilli for 1 minute. Add the beef and cook until hot.

4 Serve with the fish sauce and lime quarters.

vietnamese beef with bamboo shoots

SERVES 4

2 tbsp peanut oil

625 g/1 lb 6 oz rump steak, cut into thin strips

1 garlic clove, crushed

2.5-cm/1-inch piece grated fresh ginger

1 red chilli, deseeded and finely chopped

1 tbsp roasted sesame seeds

450 g/1 lb fresh or canned bamboo shoots, drained and rinsed

8 spring onions, chopped

2 tbsp Thai fish sauce

cooked noodles, to serve

1 Heat half the oil in a preheated wok until smoking. Add the steak strips, garlic, ginger, chilli and sesame seeds and stir-fry for 2 minutes to seal. Transfer to a plate and keep warm.

2 Heat the remaining oil in the wok and add the bamboo shoots and spring onions. Stir-fry for 3 minutes.

3 Return the steak mixture to the wok with the fish sauce and stir-fry for a further 2 minutes until heated through. Serve with freshly cooked noodles.

lamb with oyster sauce

SERVES 4

450 g/1 lb lamb leg steaks

1 tsp ground Szechuan peppercorns

1 tbsp groundnut oil

2 garlic cloves, crushed

8 spring onions, sliced

2 tbsp dark soy sauce

6 tbsp oyster sauce

175 g/6 oz Chinese leaves, sliced

prawn crackers, to serve

1 Using a sharp knife, remove any excess fat from the lamb. Slice the lamb thinly.

2 Sprinkle the ground Szechuan peppercorns over the meat and toss together until well combined.

3 Preheat a wok or frying pan and heat the oil. Add the lamb and stir-fry for about 5 minutes. Add the garlic and spring onions to the wok together with the dark soy sauce and stir-fry for 2 minutes.

4 Add the oyster sauce and Chinese leaves and stir-fry for a further 2 minutes, or until the leaves have wilted and the juices are bubbling.

5 Transfer to warmed serving bowls and serve immediately with prawn crackers.

lamb with black bean sauce

SERVES 4

**450 g/1 lb lamb neck fillet
or boneless leg of lamb
chops**

3 tbsp sunflower oil

1 red onion, sliced

1 red pepper, sliced

1 green pepper, sliced

**1 yellow or orange pepper,
sliced**

5 tbsp black bean sauce

**cooked rice or noodles,
to serve**

marinade

1 egg white, lightly beaten

4 tbsp cornflour

**1 tsp Chinese five-spice
powder**

1 Using a sharp knife, slice the lamb into very thin strips.

2 To make the marinade, mix together the egg white, cornflour and Chinese five-spice powder in a bowl. Toss the lamb strips in the mixture until evenly coated.

3 Heat the oil in a preheated wok or frying pan and stir-fry the lamb over a high heat for 5 minutes or until it crisps around the edges.

4 Add the onion and pepper slices to the wok and stir-fry for 5–6 minutes, or until the vegetables just begin to soften. Stir the black bean sauce into the mixture in the wok and heat through.

5 Transfer the lamb and sauce to warmed serving plates and serve immediately with freshly cooked rice or noodles.

lamb with satay sauce

SERVES 4

450 g/1 lb lamb loin fillet

marinade

1 tbsp mild curry paste

150 ml/5 fl oz coconut milk

2 garlic cloves, crushed

½ tsp chilli powder

½ tsp cumin

satay sauce

1 tbsp corn oil

1 onion, diced

6 tbsp crunchy peanut butter

1 tsp tomato purée

1 tsp fresh lime juice

100 ml/3½ fl oz cold water

1 Using a sharp knife, thinly slice the lamb and place in a large dish.

2 To make the marinade, mix together the curry paste, coconut milk, garlic, chilli powder and cumin in a bowl. Pour over the lamb, toss well, cover and marinate for 30 minutes.

3 To make the satay sauce, heat the oil in a large preheated wok and stir-fry the onion for 5 minutes, then reduce the heat and cook for 5 minutes. Stir in the peanut butter, tomato purée, lime juice and water. Remove from the heat and set aside.

4 Thread the lamb on to wooden skewers, reserving the marinade. Grill the lamb skewers under a hot grill for 6–8 minutes, turning once.

5 Add the reserved marinade to the wok, bring to the boil and cook for 5 minutes. Serve the lamb skewers with the marinade poured over the top and the satay sauce on the side.

thai lamb with lime leaves

SERVES 4

2 tbsp groundnut oil

2 garlic cloves, crushed

4 shallots, chopped

2 lemon grass stalks, sliced

6 kaffir lime leaves

1 tbsp tamarind paste

25 g/1 oz palm sugar

2 red chillies, deseeded and finely chopped

450 g/1 lb lean lamb (leg or loin fillet)

600 ml/1 pint coconut milk

175 g/6 oz cherry tomatoes, halved

1 tbsp chopped fresh coriander

cooked fragrant rice, to serve

1 Using a sharp knife, cut the lamb into thin strips or cubes. Heat the oil in a large preheated wok or frying pan. Add the garlic, shallots, lemon grass, lime leaves, tamarind paste, sugar and chillies and stir-fry for about 2 minutes.

2 Add the lamb to the wok or frying pan and stir-fry for about 5 minutes, tossing well so that the lamb is evenly coated in the spice mixture.

3 Pour the coconut milk into the wok or pan and bring to the boil. Reduce the heat and simmer gently for 20 minutes.

4 Add the tomatoes and coriander and simmer, stirring occasionally, for a further 5 minutes. Transfer to warmed serving plates and serve immediately with freshly cooked fragrant rice.

stir-fried lamb with orange

SERVES 4

450 g/1 lb minced lamb

2 garlic cloves, crushed

1 tsp cumin seeds

1 tsp ground coriander

1 red onion, sliced

finely grated rind and juice of 1 orange

2 tbsp soy sauce

1 orange, peeled and segmented

salt and pepper

snipped fresh chives, to garnish

1 Heat a wok or large frying pan, without adding any oil.

2 Add the minced lamb to the wok. Dry-fry the minced lamb for 5 minutes or until the lamb is evenly browned. Drain away any excess fat from the wok.

3 Add the garlic, cumin seeds, coriander and red onion to the wok and stir-fry for a further 5 minutes. Stir in the finely grated orange rind and juice and the soy sauce, mixing until thoroughly combined. Cover, reduce the heat and leave to simmer, stirring occasionally, for 15 minutes.

4 Remove the lid, increase the heat and add the orange segments. Stir to mix. Season with salt and pepper to taste and heat through for a further 2–3 minutes.

5 Transfer to warmed serving plates and garnish with snipped fresh chives. Serve immediately.

sweet & sour spare ribs

SERVES 4

450 g/1 lb spare ribs, cut into bite-sized pieces

vegetable or groundnut oil, for deep-frying, plus 1/½ tbsp, for stir-frying

1 green pepper, roughly chopped

1 small onion, roughly chopped

1 small carrot, finely sliced

½ tsp finely chopped garlic

½ tsp finely chopped fresh ginger

100 g/3½ oz pineapple chunks

marinade

2 tsp light soy sauce

½ tsp salt

pinch of white pepper

sauce

3 tbsp white rice vinegar

2 tbsp sugar

1 tbsp light soy sauce

1 tbsp tomato ketchup

1 To make the marinade, combine the marinade ingredients in a bowl with the spare ribs and marinate for at least 20 minutes.

2 Heat enough oil for deep-frying in a preheated wok or deep-fat fryer until it reaches 180–190°C/350–375°F/ Gas Mark 4–5, or until a cube of bread browns in 30 seconds. Deep-fry the spare ribs for 8 minutes. Drain and set aside.

3 To prepare the sauce, mix together the vinegar, sugar, light soy sauce and ketchup. Set aside.

4 In a preheated wok, heat 1 tablespoon of the oil and stir-fry the pepper, onion and carrot for 2 minutes. Remove and set aside. Wipe the wok clean.

5 In the clean preheated wok, heat ½ tablespoon oil and stir-fry the garlic and ginger until fragrant. Add the sauce. Bring back to the boil and add the pineapple chunks. Finally add the spare ribs and the pepper, onion and carrot. Stir until warmed through and serve immediately.

pork & crab meatballs

SERVES 6

225 g/8 oz pork fillet, finely chopped

170 g/5¾ oz canned crabmeat, drained

3 spring onions, finely chopped

1 garlic clove, finely chopped

1 tsp Thai red curry paste

1 tbsp cornflour

1 egg white

vegetable or groundnut oil, for deep-frying

cooked rice, to serve

sauce

1 tbsp vegetable or groundnut oil

2 shallots, chopped

1 garlic clove, crushed

2 large red chillies, deseeded and chopped

4 spring onions, chopped

3 tomatoes, roughly chopped

1 Put the pork and crabmeat into a bowl and mix together. Add the spring onions, garlic, curry paste, cornflour and egg white and beat together well to make a thick paste. With damp hands, shape the mixture into walnut-sized balls.

2 Heat the oil in a preheated wok and deep-fry the balls, in batches, for 3–4 minutes, turning frequently, until golden brown and cooked. Drain on kitchen paper and keep warm.

3 To make the sauce, heat the oil in a preheated wok and stir-fry the shallots and garlic for 1–2 minutes. Add the chillies and spring onions and stir-fry for 1–2 minutes, then add the tomatoes. Stir together quickly, then spoon the sauce over the pork and crab balls. Serve immediately with freshly cooked rice.

pork pad thai

SERVES 4

**225 g/8 oz thick dried rice
noodles**

**2 tbsp groundnut or
vegetable oil**

**4 spring onions, roughly
chopped**

2 garlic cloves, crushed

**2 red chillies, deseeded
and sliced**

**225 g/8 oz pork fillet,
trimmed and thinly
sliced**

**115 g/4 oz cooked peeled
large prawns**

juice of 1 lime

2 tbsp Thai fish sauce

2 eggs, beaten

55 g/2 oz fresh beansprouts

**handful of chopped fresh
coriander**

**55 g/2 oz unsalted peanuts,
chopped**

lime wedges, to serve

1 Soak the noodles in a large saucepan of boiling water,
covered, for 10 minutes until just tender, or according to
the packet instructions. Drain, rinse under cold running water
and set aside.

2 Heat the oil in a preheated wok, add the spring onions,
garlic and chillies and stir-fry over a medium–high heat
for 1–2 minutes. Add the pork and stir-fry over a high heat
for 1–2 minutes until browned all over.

3 Add the prawns, lime juice, fish sauce and eggs and stir-
fry over a medium heat for 2–3 minutes until the eggs
have set and the prawns are heated through.

4 Add the beansprouts, most of the coriander, the peanuts
and the noodles and stir-fry for 30 seconds until
heated through. Garnish with the remaining coriander and
serve immediately with lime wedges.

sweet & sour pork

150 ml/5 fl oz vegetable oil, for deep-frying

225 g/8 oz pork fillet, cut into 1-cm/½-inch cubes

1 onion, sliced

1 green pepper, sliced

225 g/8 oz pineapple pieces

1 small carrot, cut into thin strips

25 g/1 oz canned bamboo shoots, drained, rinsed and halved

cooked rice or noodles, to serve

batter

125 g/4½ oz plain flour

1 tbsp cornflour

1½ tsp baking powder

1 tbsp vegetable oil

sauce

125 g/4½ oz soft light brown sugar

2 tbsp cornflour

125 ml/4 fl oz white wine vinegar

2 garlic cloves, crushed

4 tbsp tomato purée

6 tbsp pineapple juice

1 To make the batter, sift the plain flour into a mixing bowl, together with the cornflour and baking powder. Add the vegetable oil and stir in enough water to make a thick, smooth batter (about 175 ml/6 fl oz).

2 Pour the vegetable oil into a preheated wok and heat until almost smoking.

3 Dip the cubes of pork into the batter, and cook in the hot oil, in batches, until the pork is cooked through. Remove the pork from the wok with a slotted spoon and drain on kitchen paper. Set aside and keep warm until required.

4 Drain all but 1 tablespoon of oil from the wok and return it to the heat. Add the onion, pepper, pineapple pieces, carrot and bamboo shoots and stir-fry for 1–2 minutes. Remove from the wok with a slotted spoon and set aside. Mix all of the sauce ingredients together and pour into the wok.

5 Bring to the boil, stirring until thickened and clear. Cook for 1 minute, then return the pork and vegetables to the wok. Cook for a further 1–2 minutes, then transfer to a warmed serving plate and serve with freshly cooked rice or noodles.

pork with basil & lemon grass

SERVES 4

350 g/12 oz pork tenderloin, cubed

2 tbsp sesame oil

280 g/10 oz mushrooms, thinly sliced

1 courgette, thinly sliced

2 carrots, thinly sliced

115 g/4 oz canned bamboo shoots, drained and rinsed

115 g/4 oz canned water chestnuts, thinly sliced

1 garlic clove, crushed

125 ml/4 fl oz chicken stock

lime wedges, to serve

cooked basmati rice, to serve

marinade

1 lemon grass stalk, finely sliced

2 tbsp Thai fish sauce

4 tbsp fresh basil, shredded

juice of 1 lime

1 To make the marinade, mix the lemon grass, fish sauce, basil and lime juice in a bowl. Stir in the pork and toss well to coat. Cover with clingfilm and refrigerate for 1–2 hours.

2 Heat 1 tablespoon of the oil in a preheated wok or frying pan over a medium heat. Add the meat and the marinade and stir-fry until the pork is browned. Remove from the pan, set aside and keep warm.

3 Add the remaining tablespoon of oil to the pan and heat. Add all the vegetables and the garlic and stir-fry for about 3 minutes.

4 Return the pork to the pan and add the chicken stock. Cook for 5 minutes until the stock is reduced.

5 Transfer the stir-fry to warmed serving dishes. Serve with lime wedges and freshly cooked basmati rice.

szechuan-style pork & pepper

SERVES 4

**500 g/1 lb 2 oz pork
tenderloin, cubed**

2 tbsp cornflour

3 tbsp soy sauce

1 tbsp white wine vinegar

250 ml/9 fl oz water

2 tbsp groundnut oil

2 leeks, thinly sliced

**1 red pepper, cut into thin
strips**

**1 courgette, cut into thin
strips**

1 carrot, cut into thin strips

pinch of salt

cooked wild rice, to serve

marinade

1 tbsp soy sauce

pinch of chilli flakes

1 To make the marinade, mix the soy sauce and chilli flakes in a bowl. Add the pork and toss to coat. Cover with clingfilm and leave to stand for 30 minutes.

2 Combine the cornflour, soy sauce and white wine vinegar in a small bowl. Stir in the water gradually, then set aside. Heat 1 tablespoon of the oil in a preheated wok or frying pan. Add the pork and marinade mixture and stir-fry for 2–3 minutes. Remove the pork from the pan with a slotted spoon and set aside.

3 Heat the remaining oil in the pan, add the leeks and red pepper and stir-fry for 2 minutes. Then add the courgette, carrot and salt and stir-fry for 2 more minutes.

4 Stir in the pork and the cornflour mixture and bring to the boil, stirring constantly until the sauce thickens. Remove from the heat.

5 Serve immediately with freshly cooked wild rice.

hoisin pork with garlic noodles

SERVES 4

250 g/9 oz dried thick Chinese egg noodles, or Chinese wholemeal egg noodles

450 g/1 lb pork fillet, thinly sliced

1 tsp sugar

1 tbsp groundnut or corn oil

4 tbsp rice vinegar

4 tbsp white wine vinegar

4 tbsp bottled hoisin sauce

2 spring onions, sliced on the diagonal

about 2 tbsp garlic-flavoured corn oil

2 large garlic cloves, thinly sliced

chopped fresh coriander, to garnish

1 Start by boiling the noodles for 3 minutes, until soft. Alternatively, cook according to the packet instructions. Drain well, rinse under cold water to stop the cooking and drain again, then set aside.

2 Meanwhile, sprinkle the pork slices with the sugar and use your hands to toss together. Heat a wok over a high heat. Add the oil and heat until it shimmers. Add the pork and stir-fry for about 3 minutes until the pork is cooked through and is no longer pink. Use a slotted spoon to remove the pork from the wok and keep warm. Add both vinegars to the wok and boil until they are reduced to about 5 tablespoons. Pour in the hoisin sauce with the spring onions and let it bubble until reduced by half. Add to the pork and stir together.

3 Quickly wipe out the wok and reheat. Add the garlic-flavoured oil and heat until it shimmers. Add the garlic slices and stir round for about 30 seconds, until they are golden and crisp, then use a slotted spoon to scoop them out of the wok and set aside.

4 Add the noodles to the wok and stir them round to warm them through. Divide the noodles between four plates, top with the pork and spring onion mixture and sprinkle over the garlic slices and coriander.

VARIATION
Stir 1 tablespoon of peanut butter into the pan with the hoisin sauce for an added delicious flavour. Add 55 g/2 oz cashew nut halves or peanuts to the dish before serving.

2

Perfect
Poultry

chicken fried rice

SERVES 4

½ tbsp sesame oil

6 shallots, quartered

450 g/1 lb cooked chicken meat, cubed

3 tbsp soy sauce

2 carrots, diced

1 celery stalk, diced

1 red pepper, diced

175g/6 oz fresh peas

100 g/3½ oz canned sweetcorn kernels

275 g/9¾ oz cooked long-grain rice

2 large eggs, scrambled

1 Heat the oil in a large preheated wok or frying pan over a medium heat. Add the shallots and fry until soft, then add the chicken and 2 tablespoons of the soy sauce and stir-fry for 5–6 minutes.

2 Stir in the carrots, celery, red pepper, peas and sweetcorn and stir-fry for another 5 minutes. Add the rice and stir thoroughly.

3 Finally stir in the scrambled eggs and the remaining tablespoon of soy sauce. Serve immediately.

sweet & sour chicken

SERVES 4–6

450 g/1 lb lean chicken meat, cubed

5 tbsp vegetable or groundnut oil

½ tsp crushed garlic

½ tsp finely chopped fresh ginger

1 green pepper, roughly chopped

1 onion, roughly chopped

1 carrot, finely sliced

1 tsp sesame oil

1 tbsp finely chopped spring onion

marinade

2 tsp light soy sauce

1 tsp Shaoxing rice wine

pinch of white pepper

½ tsp salt

dash of sesame oil

sauce

8 tbsp rice vinegar

4 tbsp sugar

2 tsp light soy sauce

6 tbsp tomato ketchup

1 To make the marinade, combine all the marinade ingredients in a bowl and marinate the chicken pieces for at least 20 minutes.

2 To prepare the sauce, heat the vinegar in a pan and add the sugar, light soy sauce and tomato ketchup. Stir to dissolve the sugar, then set aside.

3 In a preheated wok, heat 3 tablespoons of the oil and stir-fry the chicken until it starts to turn golden brown. Remove and set aside. Wipe the wok clean.

4 In the clean wok, heat the remaining oil and cook the garlic and ginger until fragrant. Add the vegetables and cook for 2 minutes. Add the chicken and cook for 1 minute. Finally add the sauce and sesame oil, then stir in the spring onion and serve immediately.

hot & spicy chicken with peanuts

SERVES 4

350 g/12 oz chicken breasts, skinned and cut into chunks

4 tbsp groundnut oil

1 garlic clove, finely chopped

1 tsp grated fresh ginger

3 shallots, thinly sliced

225 g/8 oz carrots, thinly sliced

1 tsp white wine vinegar

pinch of sugar

90 g/3¼ oz roasted peanuts

1 tbsp groundnut oil

coriander sprigs, to garnish

cooked rice, to serve

marinade

2 tbsp soy sauce

1 tsp chilli powder (or to taste)

1 To make the marinade, mix the soy sauce and chilli powder in a bowl. Add the chicken chunks and toss to coat. Cover with clingfilm and refrigerate for 30 minutes.

2 Heat the oil in a preheated wok or frying pan, and stir-fry the chicken until browned and well cooked. Remove from the pan, set aside and keep warm.

3 If necessary, add a little more oil to the wok, then add the garlic, ginger, shallots and carrots. Stir-fry for 2–3 minutes.

4 Return the chicken to the wok and fry until it is warmed through. Add the vinegar, sugar and peanuts, stir well and drizzle with the groundnut oil.

5 Garnish with coriander sprigs and serve immediately with freshly cooked rice.

garlic chicken with leek

SERVES 4

450 g/1 lb chicken breasts, skinned and cut into strips

1 tbsp peanut oil

6 garlic cloves, thinly sliced

2.5-cm/1-inch piece finely grated fresh ginger

200 g/7 oz leek, thinly sliced

4 spring onions, chopped

1 tbsp clear honey

marinade

2 tbsp rice wine

2 tbsp dark soy sauce

1 tsp sesame oil

1 To make the marinade, mix the rice wine, soy sauce and sesame oil in a bowl. Add the chicken strips and stir to coat.

2 Drain the chicken, reserving the marinade. Heat the peanut oil in a preheated wok or large frying pan over a high heat until smoking. Add the drained chicken and stir-fry for 3 minutes to seal.

3 Add the garlic, ginger, leek and spring onions to the pan and fry for a further 3 minutes to soften. Add the reserved marinade and honey and stir-fry for a further minute to heat through. Serve immediately.

gong bau chicken

SERVES 4

2 boneless chicken breasts, with or without skin, cut into 1-cm/½-inch cubes

1 tbsp vegetable or groundnut oil

10 dried red chillies or more, to taste, snipped into 2 or 3 pieces

1 tsp ground Szechuan peppercorn

3 garlic cloves, finely sliced

2.5-cm/1-inch piece of fresh ginger, finely sliced

1 tbsp roughly chopped spring onion, white part only

85 g/3 oz roasted peanuts

cooked rice, to serve

marinade & sauce

3 tsp light soy sauce

1 tsp Shaoxing rice wine

1½ tsp sugar

1 tsp dark soy sauce

1 tsp black Chinese rice vinegar

a few drops of sesame oil

2 tbsp chicken stock

1 To make the marinade, combine 2 teaspoons of the light soy sauce, the Shaoxing and ½ teaspoon of sugar in a bowl and marinate the chicken, covered, for at least 20 minutes. Meanwhile, to make the sauce, combine 1 teaspoon of the light soy sauce, the dark soy sauce, Chinese rice vinegar, sesame oil, stock and 1 teaspoon of sugar in a bowl and set aside.

2 In a preheated wok, heat the oil and stir-fry the chillies and Szechuan peppercorn until crisp and fragrant. Toss in the chicken pieces. When they begin to turn white, add the garlic, ginger and spring onion. Stir-fry for about 5 minutes or until the chicken is cooked.

3 Pour in the sauce, mix together thoroughly, then stir in the peanuts. Serve immediately with freshly cooked rice.

chicken with cashew nuts

SERVES 4–6

450 g/1 lb boneless chicken meat, cut into bite-sized pieces

3 dried Chinese mushrooms, soaked in warm water for 20 minutes

2 tbsp vegetable or groundnut oil

4 slices of fresh ginger

1 tsp finely chopped garlic

1 red pepper, cut into 2.5-cm/1-inch squares

85 g/3 oz roasted cashew nuts

marinade

3 tbsp light soy sauce

1 tsp Shaoxing rice wine

pinch of sugar

½ tsp salt

1 Marinate the chicken in 2 tablespoons of the light soy sauce, Shaoxing, sugar and salt for at least 20 minutes.

2 Squeeze any excess water from the mushrooms and slice finely, discarding any tough stems. Reserve the soaking water.

3 In a preheated wok, heat 1 tablespoon of the oil. Add the ginger and stir-fry until fragrant. Stir in the chicken and cook for 2 minutes or until it begins to turn brown. Before the chicken is cooked through, remove and set aside. Wipe the wok clean.

4 In the clean wok, heat the remaining oil and stir-fry the garlic until fragrant. Add the mushrooms and red pepper and stir-fry for 1 minute. Add about 2 tablespoons of the mushroom soaking water and cook for about 2 minutes or until the water has evaporated.

5 Return the chicken to the wok, then add the remaining light soy sauce and the cashew nuts and stir-fry for 2 minutes or until the chicken is cooked through.

chicken & shiitake mushrooms

SERVES 4

2 tbsp vegetable oil

675 g/1 lb 8 oz chicken breast, skinned and cut into 2.5-cm/1-inch chunks

1 tsp grated fresh ginger

3 carrots, thinly sliced

2 onions, thinly sliced

100 g/3½ oz beansprouts

225 g/8 oz fresh or dried shiitake mushrooms, thinly sliced

3 tbsp chopped fresh coriander

cooked rice noodles, to serve

sauce

175 g/6 oz white sugar

225 ml/8 fl oz soy sauce

1 tsp Chinese five-spice powder

225 ml/8 fl oz sweet sherry

1 To make the sauce, combine the sugar, soy sauce, Chinese five-spice powder and sweet sherry in a bowl. Mix well and set aside.

2 In a preheated wok or frying pan, heat the oil over a medium–high heat. Add the chicken and stir-fry for 2 minutes, then add the ginger and fry for 1 minute, stirring constantly. Add the sauce and cook for 2 more minutes.

3 One at a time, add the carrots, onions, beansprouts, mushrooms and coriander. Stir-fry after each addition.

4 Once the sauce has reduced and is thick, transfer the stir-fry to warmed serving bowls. Serve immediately with freshly cooked rice noodles.

chicken chow mein

SERVES 4

250 g/9 oz dried medium Chinese egg noodles

2 tbsp sunflower oil

280 g/10 oz cooked chicken breasts, shredded

1 garlic clove, finely chopped

1 red pepper, thinly sliced

100 g/3½ oz shiitake mushrooms, sliced

6 spring onions, sliced

100 g/3½ oz beansprouts

3 tbsp soy sauce

1 tbsp sesame oil

1 Place the noodles in a large bowl or dish and break them up slightly. Pour enough boiling water over the noodles to cover and set aside while preparing the other ingredients.

2 In a preheated wok or frying pan, heat the oil over a medium heat. Add the shredded chicken, garlic, red pepper, mushrooms, spring onions and beansprouts to the wok and stir-fry for about 5 minutes.

3 Drain the noodles thoroughly then add them to the wok, toss well and stir-fry for a further 5 minutes. Drizzle over the soy sauce and sesame oil and toss until thoroughly combined. Transfer to warmed serving bowls and serve immediately.

ginger chicken with sesame seeds

SERVES 4

500 g/1 lb 2 oz chicken breasts, skinned and cut into strips

2 tbsp groundnut oil

1 leek, thinly sliced

1 head of broccoli, cut into small florets

2 carrots, thinly sliced

½ cauliflower, cut into small florets

1 tsp grated fresh ginger

5 tbsp white wine

2 tbsp sesame seeds

1 tbsp cornflour

1 tbsp water

cooked rice, to serve

marinade

4 tbsp soy sauce

4 tbsp water

1 To make the marinade, combine the soy sauce with 4 tablespoons of water in a medium-sized dish. Toss and coat the chicken strips in the sauce. Cover the dish with clingfilm and refrigerate for 1 hour.

2 Remove the chicken from the marinade with a slotted spoon. Heat the oil in a preheated wok or frying pan, and stir-fry the chicken and leek until the chicken is browned and the leek is beginning to soften.

3 Stir in the vegetables, ginger and wine. Reduce the heat, cover and simmer for 5 minutes. Place the sesame seeds on a baking sheet under a hot grill until lightly toasted. Stir them once to make sure they toast evenly. Set aside to cool.

4 In a small bowl, combine the cornflour with 1 tablespoon of water and whisk until smooth. Gradually add the liquid to the frying pan, stirring constantly until thickened.

5 Pile the stir-fry on to a bed of freshly cooked rice, top with the sesame seeds and serve immediately.

yaki soba

SERVES 2

400 g/14 oz ramen noodles

1 onion, finely sliced

200 g/7 oz beansprouts

**1 red pepper,
finely shredded**

**about 150 g/5½ oz cooked
chicken breast, sliced**

12 cooked peeled prawns

1 tbsp oil

**2 tbsp shoyu (Japanese soy
sauce)**

½ tbsp mirin

1 tsp sesame oil

**1 tsp sesame seeds,
roasted, to garnish**

**2 spring onions, finely
sliced, to garnish**

1 Cook the noodles according to the packet instructions, drain well and tip into a bowl.

2 Mix the onion, beansprouts, red pepper, chicken and prawns together in a separate bowl. Stir through the noodles.

3 Preheat a wok over high heat. Add the oil and heat until very hot. Add the noodle mixture and stir-fry for 4 minutes, or until golden, then add the shoyu, mirin and sesame oil and toss together.

4 Divide the mixture between two plates, garnish with the sesame seeds and spring onions and serve immediately.

chicken with pistachio nuts

SERVES 4

450 g/1 lb chicken breast, skinned and cut into strips

450 g/1 lb mushrooms, thinly sliced

1 head of broccoli, cut into florets

150 g/5½ oz beansprouts

100 g/3½ oz canned water chestnuts, drained and thinly sliced

175 g/6 oz pistachio nuts, plus extra to garnish

cooked rice, to serve

marinade

1 egg white, beaten

½ tsp salt

4 tbsp groundnut or vegetable oil

2 tsp cornflour

sauce

50 ml/2 fl oz chicken stock

2 tbsp soy sauce

2 tbsp dry sherry

1 tsp cornflour

1 To make the sauce, combine the chicken stock, soy sauce and sherry with 1 teaspoon of cornflour. Stir well and set aside.

2 To make the marinade, combine the egg white, salt, 2 tablespoons of the oil and 2 teaspoons of cornflour. Toss and coat the chicken in the mixture.

3 In a preheated wok or frying pan, heat the remaining oil until hot. Add the chicken in batches and stir-fry until golden. Remove from the wok, drain on kitchen paper and set aside to keep warm.

4 Add more oil to the wok if needed and stir-fry the mushrooms, then add the broccoli and cook for 2–3 minutes.

5 Return the chicken to the wok and add the beansprouts, water chestnuts and pistachio nuts. Stir-fry until all the ingredients are thoroughly warm. Add the sauce and cook, stirring constantly until thickened. Serve immediately over freshly cooked rice, garnished with pistachios.

warm chicken & mango salad

SERVES 4

1 tbsp groundnut oil

600 g/1lb 5 oz chicken breast, skinned and cut into strips

280 g/10 oz green beans, trimmed and cut into 2.5-cm/1-inch lengths

280 g/10 oz Chinese leaves, finely shredded

4 tbsp chopped fresh coriander

85 g/3 oz salted peanuts, roasted and chopped finely

1 mango, peeled, stoned and diced

dressing

2 tbsp Thai fish sauce

1 tbsp clear honey

4 tbsp lemon juice

1 red chilli, deseeded and finely chopped

1 Heat the oil in a preheated wok or large frying pan until smoking. Add the chicken strips and stir-fry for 2 minutes to seal. Add the green beans, reduce the heat, cover and cook for a further 5 minutes, stirring halfway through to prevent burning. Keep warm by covering with a lid.

2 Meanwhile, prepare the dressing by mixing the fish sauce, honey, lemon juice and chopped chilli together in a small bowl. Set aside.

3 Toss the Chinese leaves, coriander and chopped peanuts together in a large serving bowl.

4 Add the diced mango, warm chicken and green beans to the serving bowl, then pour over reserved dressing. Toss to coat and serve immediately.

red chicken salad

SERVES 4

4 skinless, boneless chicken breasts

2 tbsp Thai red curry paste

2 tbsp vegetable or groundnut oil

1 head Chinese leaves, shredded

175 g/6 oz bok choi, torn into large pieces

½ savoy cabbage, shredded

2 shallots, finely chopped

2 garlic cloves, crushed

1 tbsp rice wine vinegar

2 tbsp sweet chilli sauce

2 tbsp Thai soy sauce

1 Score the chicken several times and rub the curry paste into each cut. Cover and chill overnight.

2 When ready, dry-fry the chicken in a preheated wok over a medium heat for 5–6 minutes, turning once or twice, until cooked through. Set aside and keep warm.

3 Heat 1 tablespoon of the oil in a wok and stir-fry the Chinese leaves, bok choi and cabbage until just wilted. Add the remaining oil, shallots and garlic, and stir-fry until just tender but not browned. Add the vinegar, chilli sauce and soy sauce. Remove from the heat.

4 Arrange the stir-fried leaves on four serving plates. Slice the chicken, arrange on top and drizzle the hot dressing from the wok over the dish. Serve immediately.

gingered chicken & vegetable salad

SERVES 4

4 skinless, boneless chicken breasts

1 tbsp vegetable or groundnut oil

1 onion, sliced

2 garlic cloves, chopped

115 g/4 oz baby sweetcorn, halved

115 g/4 oz mangetout, halved lengthways

1 red pepper, sliced

7.5-cm/3-inch piece cucumber, peeled, deseeded and sliced

4 tbsp Thai soy sauce

1 tbsp jaggery or soft light brown sugar

few Thai basil leaves

175 g/6 oz fine egg noodles

marinade

4 spring onions, chopped

2.5-cm/1-inch piece fresh ginger, finely chopped

2 garlic cloves, crushed

2 tbsp vegetable or groundnut oil

1 Cut the chicken into large cubes, each about 2.5 cm/ 1 inch. To make the marinade, mix the spring onions, ginger, garlic and oil together in a shallow dish and add the chicken. Cover and marinate for at least 3 hours. Lift the meat out of the marinade and set aside.

2 Heat the oil in a preheated wok and cook the onion for 1–2 minutes. Add the garlic and the rest of the vegetables, except the cucumber, and cook for 2–3 minutes until just tender. Add the cucumber, half the soy sauce, the sugar and the basil, and mix gently.

3 Soak the noodles for 2–3 minutes (check the packet instructions) or until tender and drain well. Sprinkle the remaining soy sauce over them and arrange on plates. Top with the cooked vegetables.

4 Add a little more oil to the wok if necessary and cook the chicken over fairly high heat until browned on all sides. Arrange the chicken cubes on top of the salad and serve hot or warm.

chicken san choy bau

MAKES 6

1 tbsp vegetable or groundnut oil

100 g/3½ oz cooked chicken, finely chopped

25 g/1 oz water chestnuts, finely chopped

1 tsp finely chopped Chinese chives

25 g/1 oz pine nuts, lightly toasted

1 tsp salt

½ tsp white pepper

6 lettuce leaves, washed

3 tsp plum sauce, to serve

1 In a preheated wok, heat the oil and stir-fry the chicken for 1 minute. Add the water chestnuts and chives and cook for 2 minutes. Add the pine nuts and cook for 1 minute. Add the salt and pepper and stir.

2 To serve, place a spoonful of the mixture in the centre of each lettuce leaf, then top with the plum sauce and fold the lettuce leaf to make a small roll.

stir-fried turkey with cranberry glaze

SERVES 4

450g/1 lb boneless turkey breast

2 tbsp sunflower oil

15 g/½ oz stem ginger

50 g/1¾ oz fresh or frozen cranberries

100 g/3½ oz canned chestnuts

4 tbsp cranberry sauce

3 tbsp light soy sauce

salt and pepper

1 Remove any skin from the turkey breast. Using a sharp knife, thinly slice the turkey breast.

2 Heat the sunflower oil in a large preheated wok or frying pan. Add the turkey to the wok and stir-fry for 5 minutes, or until cooked through. Drain off the syrup from the stem ginger. Using a sharp knife, chop the ginger finely.

3 Add the ginger and the cranberries to the wok and stir-fry for 2–3 minutes, or until the cranberries have softened. Add the chestnuts, cranberry sauce and soy sauce, season to taste with salt and pepper and allow to bubble for 2–3 minutes.

4 Transfer to warmed serving dishes and serve immediately.

lemon turkey
with spinach

SERVES 4

450 g/1 lb turkey breast, skinned and cut into strips

1 tbsp vegetable oil

6 spring onions, finely sliced

½ lemon, peeled and thinly sliced

1 garlic clove, finely chopped

300 g/10½ oz spinach, washed, drained and roughly chopped

3 tbsp chopped fresh flat-leaf parsley

cooked pasta, to serve

sprigs of flat-leaf parsley, to garnish

lemon slices, to garnish

marinade

1 tbsp soy sauce

1 tbsp white wine vinegar

1 tsp cornflour

1 tsp finely grated lemon zest

½ tsp finely ground black pepper

1 To make the marinade, put the soy sauce, vinegar, cornflour, lemon zest and pepper in a bowl and mix thoroughly. Add the turkey and stir to coat. Cover with clingfilm and marinate in the refrigerator for 30 minutes.

2 Heat the oil in a large preheated wok or frying pan. Add the turkey and the marinade and cook over a medium heat for 2–3 minutes or until the turkey is opaque.

3 Add the spring onions, lemon slivers and garlic and cook for another 2–3 minutes. Stir in the spinach and parsley and cook until the spinach is just wilted.

4 Remove from the heat, spoon over freshly cooked pasta and garnish with sprigs of parsley and lemon slices before serving.

turkey, broccoli & bok choi

SERVES 4

450 g/1 lb turkey breast, skinned and cut into strips

1 tbsp vegetable oil

1 head of broccoli, cut into florets

2 heads of bok choi leaves, washed and separated (or savoy cabbage, if preferred)

1 red pepper, thinly sliced

50 ml/2 fl oz chicken stock

cooked rice, to serve

marinade

1 tbsp soy sauce

1 tbsp honey

2 garlic cloves, crushed

1 To make the marinade, combine the soy sauce, honey and garlic in a medium-sized bowl. Add the turkey and toss to coat. Cover the bowl with clingfilm and marinate in the refrigerator for 2 hours.

2 Preheat a wok or large frying pan over a medium–high heat and add the oil; heat for 1 minute. Add the turkey and stir-fry for 3 minutes or until the turkey is opaque. Remove with a slotted spoon, set aside and keep warm.

3 Add the broccoli, bok choi (or savoy cabbage) and the pepper to the pan and stir-fry for 2 minutes. Add the stock and continue to stir-fry for 2 minutes or until the vegetables are crisp yet tender.

4 Return the turkey to the wok and cook briefly to reheat. Serve immediately with freshly cooked rice.

turkey with bamboo shoots

SERVES 4

450 g/1 lb turkey breast, skinned and cubed

1 tbsp sesame oil

125 g/4½ oz small mushrooms, cut into halves

1 green pepper, cut into strips

1 courgette, thinly sliced

4 spring onions, cut into quarters

115 g/4 oz canned bamboo shoots, drained and rinsed

115 g/4 oz canned water chestnuts, sliced

lemon wedges, to serve

marinade

4 tbsp sweet sherry

1 tbsp lemon juice

1 tbsp soy sauce

2 tsp grated fresh ginger

1 garlic clove, crushed

1 To make the marinade, combine the sherry, lemon juice, soy sauce, ginger and garlic in a bowl, then add the turkey and stir. Cover the dish with clingfilm and marinate in the refrigerator for 3–4 hours.

2 In a preheated wok or frying pan, add the oil and heat slowly. Remove the turkey from the marinade with a slotted spoon (reserving the marinade) and stir-fry a few pieces at a time until browned. Remove the turkey from the wok and set aside.

3 Add the mushrooms, green pepper and courgette to the wok and stir-fry for 3 minutes. Add the spring onions and stir-fry for 1 minute more. Add the bamboo shoots and water chestnuts to the wok, then the turkey along with half of the reserved marinade. Stir over a medium–high heat for another 2–3 minutes until the ingredients are evenly coated and the marinade has reduced.

4 Serve immediately in warmed bowls with lemon wedges on the side.

honeyed duck

SERVES 4

4 skinless duck breasts, sliced

1 tbsp olive oil

bunch of spring onions, trimmed and sliced

1 small head Chinese cabbage, finely shredded

salt and pepper

marinade

2 tbsp clear honey

4 tbsp soy sauce

1 To make the marinade, mix the honey and soy sauce together in a large bowl. Add the duck slices and toss to coat in the mixture.

2 Heat the oil in a preheated wok or frying pan. Add the duck strips (reserving the marinade) and cook for 2 minutes until browned.

3 Add the spring onions, Chinese cabbage and the reserved marinade. Cook for 3–4 minutes until the duck is cooked but still a little pink in the centre.

4 Season with salt and pepper and serve immediately.

duck salad

SERVES 4

4 boneless duck breasts, skin on

½ fresh pineapple, peeled and sliced

7.5-cm/3-inch piece cucumber, peeled, deseeded and sliced

3 tomatoes, cut into wedges

1 onion, thinly sliced

marinade

1 lemon grass stalk, broken into three and each cut in half lengthways

3 tbsp vegetable or groundnut oil

2 tbsp sesame oil

1 tsp Thai fish sauce

1 green chilli, deseeded and chopped

2 tbsp Thai red curry paste

dressing

juice of 1 lemon

2 garlic cloves, crushed

1 tsp jaggery or soft light brown sugar

2 tbsp vegetable or groundnut oil

1 Unwrap the duck and let the skin dry out overnight in the refrigerator.

2 The following day, slash the skin side five or six times. To make the marinade, mix the lemon grass, 2 tablespoons of the oil, all the sesame oil, fish sauce, chilli and curry paste together in a shallow dish and place the duck breasts in the mixture. Turn to coat and rub the marinade into the meat. Chill for 2–3 hours.

3 Heat the remaining oil in a preheated wok and cook the duck, skin-side down, over medium heat for 3–4 minutes until the skin is browned and crisp and the meat cooked most of the way through. Turn the breasts over and cook until browned and the meat is cooked to your liking.

4 Meanwhile, arrange the pineapple, cucumber, tomatoes and onions on a platter. Mix the dressing ingredients together and pour over the top.

5 Lift the duck out of the wok and slice thickly. Arrange the duck slices on top of the salad and serve immediately.

duck & pea stir-fry

SERVES 4

450 g/1 lb skinless, boneless duck breasts

3 tbsp groundnut oil

6 large spring onions, white and green parts separated, diagonally sliced into 2-cm/¾-inch pieces

1 tsp finely chopped fresh ginger

300 g/10½ oz mangetout, halved diagonally

140 g/5 oz shelled peas

3 tbsp whole almonds with skin, halved lengthways

55 g/2 oz fresh beansprouts

cooked noodles, to serve

marinade

1 tbsp soft light brown sugar

3 tbsp warm water

1–2 red chillies, deseeded and very finely chopped

1 tbsp soy sauce

1 tsp Thai fish sauce

3 tbsp lime juice

1 Combine the marinade ingredients in a bowl, stirring to dissolve the sugar. Slice the duck into bite-sized pieces and add to the marinade. Leave to stand at room temperature for 30 minutes, or overnight in the refrigerator.

2 Heat a wok over a high heat, then add the oil. Add the white spring onion and the ginger and stir-fry for a few seconds. Add the duck and the marinade, and stir-fry for about 5 minutes. When the liquid has reduced slightly, add the mangetout and peas and stir-fry for a further 2–3 minutes.

3 Add the almonds, beansprouts and green spring onion, and stir-fry for a few seconds to heat through. Serve immediately with freshly cooked noodles.

duck with mixed peppers

SERVES 4

1 tbsp vegetable or groundnut oil

2 duck breasts, skin on

1 onion, sliced

2 garlic cloves, chopped

1 red pepper, chopped

1 green pepper, chopped

1 yellow pepper, chopped

4 tomatoes, peeled, deseeded and chopped

150 ml/5 fl oz stock

3 tbsp Thai soy sauce

cooked noodles, garnished with chopped onion, to serve

1 Heat the oil in a preheated wok and cook the duck breasts over a high heat until crisp and brown. Turn over and cook until cooked through. Lift out and keep warm.

2 Pour off any excess fat and stir-fry the onion and garlic for 2–3 minutes until softened and lightly browned.

3 Add the peppers and stir-fry for 2–3 minutes until tender. Add the tomatoes, stock and soy sauce and simmer for 1–2 minutes. Transfer to a warmed serving plate. Slice the duck thickly and arrange on top, spooning any sauce over it. Serve with freshly cooked noodles garnished with chopped onion.

fruity duck stir-fry

SERVES 4

4 duck breasts, skinned and cut into thin slices

1 tbsp chilli oil

225 g/8 oz baby onions, peeled

2 garlic cloves, crushed

100 g/3½ oz baby sweetcorn

175 g/6 oz canned pineapple chunks

6 spring onions, sliced

100 g/3½ oz beansprouts

2 tbsp plum sauce

marinade

1 tsp Chinese five-spice powder

1 tbsp cornflour

1 To make the marinade, mix the Chinese five-spice powder and the cornflour in a bowl. Toss the duck in the mixture until well coated.

2 Heat the oil in a preheated wok. Stir-fry the duck for 10 minutes or until just beginning to crisp around the edges. Remove from the wok and set aside.

3 Add the onions and garlic to the wok and stir-fry for 5 minutes or until softened. Add the baby sweetcorn and stir-fry for a further 5 minutes. Add the pineapple, spring onions and beansprouts and stir-fry for 3–4 minutes. Stir in the plum sauce.

4 Return the cooked duck to the wok and toss until well mixed. Transfer to warmed serving dishes and serve immediately.

VARIATION

Replace the canned pineapple chunks with the same amount of kumquats, washed and chopped into small chunks.

3

Flavoursome Fish & Seafood

fish in coconut

SERVES 4

2 tbsp vegetable or groundnut oil

6 spring onions, roughly chopped

2.5-cm/1-inch piece grated fresh ginger

2–3 tbsp Thai red curry paste

400 ml/14 fl oz coconut milk

150 ml/5 fl oz fish stock

4 kaffir lime leaves

1 lemon grass stalk, broken in half

350 g/12 oz white fish fillets, skinned and cut into chunks

225 g/8 oz squid rings and tentacles

225 g/8 oz large cooked peeled prawns

1 tbsp Thai fish sauce

2 tbsp Thai soy sauce

4 tbsp chopped fresh Chinese chives

cooked jasmine rice with chopped fresh coriander, to serve

1 Heat the oil in a preheated wok and stir-fry the spring onions and ginger for 1–2 minutes. Add the curry paste and stir-fry for 1–2 minutes.

2 Add the coconut milk, fish stock, lime leaves and lemon grass. Bring to the boil, then reduce the heat and simmer for 1 minute.

3 Add the fish, squid and prawns, and simmer for 2–3 minutes until the fish is cooked. Add the fish sauce and soy sauce and stir in the chives. Serve immediately, accompanied by freshly cooked jasmine rice with fresh coriander stirred through it.

five-willow fish

SERVES 4–6

1 whole sea bass or similar, weighing 450–675 g/ 1–1 lb 8 oz, gutted

2 tsp salt

6 tbsp vegetable or groundnut oil

2 slices fresh ginger

2 garlic cloves, finely sliced

2 spring onions, roughly chopped

1 green pepper, thinly sliced

1 red pepper, thinly sliced

1 carrot, finely sliced

55 g/2 oz fresh or canned bamboo shoots, drained, rinsed and thinly sliced (if using fresh shoots, boil in water first for 30 minutes)

2 tomatoes, peeled, deseeded and thinly sliced

1 tbsp Shaoxing rice wine

2 tbsp white rice vinegar

1 tbsp light soy sauce

1 tbsp sugar

1 Clean the fish and dry thoroughly. Score the fish on both sides with deep, diagonal cuts. Press ½ teaspoon of the salt into the skin.

2 In a preheated wok, heat 4 tablespoons of the oil and cook the fish for about 4 minutes on each side or until the flesh is soft. Drain, then set aside on a warmed dish and keep warm. Wipe the wok clean.

3 Preheat the clean wok and heat the remaining oil and stir-fry the ginger, garlic and spring onions until fragrant. Toss in the vegetables with the remaining salt and stir rapidly for 2–3 minutes. Add the remaining ingredients and mix well for 2–3 minutes. Pour the sauce over the fish and serve immediately.

monkfish stir-fry

SERVES 4

2 tsp sesame oil

450 g/1 lb monkfish steaks, cut into 2.5-cm/1-inch chunks

1 onion, thinly sliced

3 garlic cloves, finely chopped

1 tsp grated fresh ginger

225 g/8 oz fine tip asparagus

175 g/6 oz mushrooms, thinly sliced

2 tbsp soy sauce

1 tbsp lemon juice

lemon wedges, to serve

cooked noodles, to serve

1 Heat the oil in a preheated wok or frying pan over a medium–high heat. Add the fish, onion, garlic, ginger, asparagus and mushrooms. Stir-fry for 2–3 minutes.

2 Stir in the soy sauce and lemon juice and cook for another minute. Remove from the heat and transfer to warmed serving dishes.

3 Serve immediately with lemon wedges over freshly cooked noodles.

indian monkfish & okra

SERVES 4

750 g/1 lb 10 oz monkfish fillet, cut into 3-cm/ 1¼-inch cubes

250 g/9 oz okra

2 tbsp sunflower oil

1 onion, sliced

1 garlic clove, crushed

2.5-cm/1-inch piece fresh ginger, sliced

150 ml/5 fl oz coconut milk or fish stock

2 tsp garam masala

fresh coriander sprigs, to garnish

4 lime wedges, to serve

marinade

3 tbsp lemon juice

grated rind of 1 lemon

¼ tsp aniseed

½ tsp salt

½ tsp pepper

1 To make the marinade, mix the ingredients together in a bowl. Stir the monkfish into the bowl and leave to marinate for 1 hour.

2 Bring a saucepan of water to the boil, add the okra and boil for 4–5 minutes. Drain and cut the okra into 1-cm/½-inch slices.

3 Heat the oil in a preheated wok, add the onion and stir-fry until golden brown. Add the garlic and ginger and fry for 1 minute. Add the fish with the marinade and stir-fry for 2 minutes.

4 Stir in the okra, coconut milk or fish stock and the garam masala and simmer for 10 minutes. Serve with lime wedges and garnish with coriander sprigs.

fried fish with pine nuts

SERVES 4–6

½ tsp salt

450 g/1 lb thick white fish fillets, cut into 2.5-cm/ 1-inch cubes

2 dried Chinese mushrooms, soaked in warm water for 20 minutes

3 tbsp vegetable or groundnut oil

2.5-cm/1-inch piece fresh ginger, finely shredded

1 tbsp chopped spring onion

1 red pepper, cut into 2.5-cm/1-inch squares

1 green pepper, cut into 2.5-cm/1-inch squares

25 g/1 oz fresh or canned bamboo shoots, drained, rinsed and cut into small cubes (if using fresh shoots, boil in water first for 30 minutes)

2 tsp Shaoxing rice wine

2 tbsp pine nuts, toasted, to garnish

cooked rice, to serve

1 Sprinkle the salt over the fish and set aside for 20 minutes. Squeeze out any excess water from the mushrooms and slice finely, discarding any tough stems.

2 In a preheated wok, heat 2 tablespoons of the oil and fry the fish for 3 minutes. Drain the fish, set aside and then wipe the wok clean.

3 Preheat the clean wok, heat the remaining oil and toss in the ginger. Stir until fragrant, then add the spring onion, peppers, bamboo shoots, mushrooms and Shaoxing and cook for 1–2 minutes.

4 Finally, add the fish and stir to warm through. Garnish with pine nuts and serve with freshly cooked rice.

chillies stuffed with fish paste

SERVES 4–6

225 g/8 oz white fish, minced

2 tbsp lightly beaten egg

4–6 mild large red and green chillies

vegetable or groundnut oil, for shallow-frying

2 garlic cloves, finely chopped

½–1 tsp fermented black beans, rinsed and lightly mashed

1 tbsp light soy sauce

pinch of sugar

1 tbsp water

marinade

1 tsp finely chopped fresh ginger

pinch of salt

pinch of white pepper

½ tsp vegetable or groundnut oil

1 To make the marinade, combine all the ingredients in a bowl and marinate the fish for 20 minutes. Add the egg and mix by hand to create a smooth paste.

2 To prepare the chillies, cut in half lengthways and scoop out the seeds and loose flesh. Cut into bite-sized pieces. Spread each piece of chilli with about ½ teaspoon of the fish paste.

3 In a preheated wok, heat plenty of the oil and cook the chilli pieces on both sides until beginning to turn golden brown. Drain the chillies, set aside and wipe the wok clean.

4 Heat 1 tablespoon of fresh oil in the clean wok and stir-fry the garlic until aromatic. Stir in the black beans and mix well. Add the light soy sauce and sugar and stir, then add the chilli pieces. Add the water, then cover and simmer over low heat for 5 minutes. Serve immediately.

salmon & scallops with coriander & lime

SERVES 4

6 tbsp groundnut oil

280 g/10 oz salmon steak, skinned and cut into 2.5-cm/1-inch chunks

225 g/8 oz scallops

3 carrots, thinly sliced

2 celery stalks, cut into 2.5-cm/1-inch pieces

2 yellow peppers, thinly sliced

175 g/6 oz oyster mushrooms, thinly sliced

1 garlic clove, crushed

6 tbsp chopped fresh coriander

3 shallots, thinly sliced

juice of 2 limes

1 tsp lime zest

1 tsp dried red pepper flakes

3 tbsp dry sherry

3 tbsp soy sauce

cooked noodles, to serve

1 In a large preheated wok or frying pan, heat the oil over a medium heat. Add the salmon and scallops, and stir-fry for 3 minutes. Remove from the wok, set aside and keep warm.

2 Add the carrots, celery, peppers, mushrooms and garlic to the wok and stir-fry for 3 minutes. Add the coriander and shallots and stir.

3 Add the lime juice and zest, dried red pepper flakes, sherry and soy sauce and stir. Return the salmon and scallops to the wok and stir-fry carefully for another minute.

4 Serve immediately over freshly cooked noodles.

mackerel with ginger

SERVES 2–3

4 mackerel fillets with skin, weighing about 450 g/1 lb in total

1 tsp finely chopped fresh ginger, plus 2.5 cm/1-inch piece finely shredded lengthways

½ tsp salt

4 tbsp groundnut oil

2½ tbsp plain flour

3 spring onions, green parts included, sliced

finely shredded Chinese leaves, to garnish

sauce

2 tbsp light soy sauce

½ tsp sugar

2 tsp Chinese rice wine or dry sherry

1 Slice the mackerel fillets in half crossways. Diagonally slash the skin of each piece once or twice. Combine the teaspoon of chopped ginger with the salt. Rub the mixture over both sides of the fish, rubbing it into the slashes and any crevices in the flesh. Leave to stand for 15 minutes.

2 Combine the sauce ingredients in a small bowl and set aside.

3 Heat a wok over a medium–high heat and add the oil. Dredge the mackerel fillets in the flour and add to the wok. Fry for 4 minutes, turning once. Pour the sauce over the fish, sprinkle with the shredded ginger and spring onions, and fry for a further 2 minutes.

4 Transfer to a warmed serving dish and garnish with a few shreds of Chinese leaves. Serve immediately.

spicy thai seafood stew

SERVES 4

200 g/7 oz squid, cleaned and tentacles discarded

500 g/1 lb 2 oz firm white fish fillet, preferably monkfish or halibut

1 tbsp corn oil

4 shallots, finely chopped

2 garlic cloves, finely chopped

2 tbsp Thai green curry paste

2 small lemon grass stems, finely chopped

1 tsp shrimp paste

500 ml/18 fl oz coconut milk

200 g/7 oz raw king prawns, peeled and deveined

12 live clams in shells, cleaned

8 fresh basil leaves, finely shredded, plus extra whole leaves to garnish

cooked rice, to serve

1 Using a sharp knife, cut the squid body cavities into thick rings and the white fish into bite-sized chunks.

2 Heat the oil in a large preheated wok. Add the shallots, garlic and curry paste and stir-fry for 1–2 minutes. Add the lemon grass and shrimp paste, then stir in the coconut milk and bring to the boil.

3 Reduce the heat until the liquid is simmering gently, then add the squid, white fish and prawns to the wok and simmer for 2 minutes.

4 Add the clams and simmer for a further 1 minute or until the clams have opened. Discard any clams that remain closed.

5 Sprinkle the shredded basil leaves over the stew. Transfer to warmed serving plates, then garnish with whole basil leaves and serve immediately with freshly cooked rice.

stir-fried squid with hot black bean sauce

SERVES 4

750 g/1 lb 10 oz squid, cleaned and tentacles discarded

1 large red pepper, deseeded

115 g/4 oz mangetout

1 head of bok choi

1½ tbsp corn oil

1 small red bird's-eye chilli, chopped

1 garlic clove, finely chopped

1 tsp grated fresh ginger

2 spring onions, chopped

sauce

3 tbsp black bean sauce

1 tbsp Thai fish sauce

1 tbsp rice wine or dry sherry

1 tbsp dark soy sauce

1 tsp brown sugar

1 tsp cornflour

1 tbsp water

1 Cut the squid body cavities into quarters lengthways. Use the tip of a small, sharp knife to score a diamond pattern into the flesh without cutting all the way through. Pat dry with kitchen paper.

2 Cut the pepper into long, thin slices. Cut the mangetout in half diagonally. Coarsely shred the bok choi.

3 To make the sauce, mix the black bean sauce, fish sauce, rice wine, soy sauce and sugar together in a bowl. Blend the cornflour with the water and stir into the other ingredients in the bowl. Reserve the mixture until required.

4 Heat the oil in a preheated wok. Add the chilli, garlic, ginger and spring onions and stir-fry for 1 minute. Add the pepper slices and stir-fry for 2 minutes.

5 Add the squid and stir-fry over a high heat for a further 1 minute. Stir in the mangetout and bok choi and stir for a further 1 minute or until wilted. Stir in the sauce ingredients and cook, stirring constantly, for 2 minutes or until the sauce thickens and clears. Serve immediately.

sweet chilli squid

SERVES 4

2 tbsp sesame oil

280 g/10 oz squid, cleaned, tentacles discarded and cut into strips

2 red peppers, thinly sliced

3 shallots, thinly sliced

85 g/3 oz mushrooms, thinly sliced

1 tbsp dry sherry

4 tbsp soy sauce

1 tsp sugar

1 tsp hot chilli flakes, or to taste

1 garlic clove, crushed

1 tbsp sesame seeds, toasted

1 tsp sesame oil

cooked rice, to serve

1 Heat 1 tablespoon of oil in a preheated wok over a medium heat. Add the squid and cook for 2 minutes. Remove from the wok and set aside.

2 Add the other tablespoon of oil to the wok and stir-fry the peppers and shallots over a medium heat for 1 minute. Add the mushrooms and stir-fry for another 2 minutes.

3 Return the squid to the wok and add the sherry, soy sauce, sugar, chilli flakes and garlic, stirring thoroughly. Cook for a further 2 minutes.

4 Sprinkle with the toasted sesame seeds, drizzle over 1 teaspoon sesame oil and mix. Serve on a bed of freshly cooked rice.

ginger squid & prawn stir-fry

SERVES 4

175 g/6 oz squid, cleaned, tentacles discarded and cut into thick rings

250 g/9 oz raw king prawns, peeled and cut in half lengthways

2 spring onions, finely sliced

2.5-cm/1-inch piece finely grated fresh ginger

2 garlic cloves, finely chopped

2 tbsp fresh lemon juice

2 tbsp Thai sweet chilli dipping sauce

2 tbsp sunflower oil

200 g/7 oz small head of broccoli florets

140 g/5 oz mangetout, halved diagonally

1 Mix together the squid rings, halved prawns, spring onion, ginger, garlic, lemon juice, chilli sauce and half the oil in a bowl. Leave to marinate for 30 minutes.

2 Heat the remaining oil in a preheated wok and stir-fry the broccoli for 2 minutes. Add the mangetout and stir-fry with the broccoli for a further minute.

3 Add the squid and prawn mixture and cook for 3 minutes until the prawns are pink.

4 Spoon into a warmed dish and serve immediately.

prawn fu yung

SERVES 4–6

**1 tbsp vegetable or
groundnut oil**

**115 g/4 oz raw prawns,
peeled and deveined**

4 eggs, lightly beaten

1 tsp salt

pinch of white pepper

**2 tbsp finely chopped
Chinese chives**

1 In a preheated wok, heat the oil and stir-fry the prawns
until they begin to turn pink.

2 Season the beaten eggs with the salt and pepper and
pour over the prawns. Stir-fry for 1 minute, then add
the chives.

3 Cook for a further 4 minutes, stirring all the time, until
the eggs are cooked through but still soft in texture, and
serve immediately.

prawns, mangetout & cashew nuts

SERVES 4

85 g/3 oz dry roasted cashew nuts

3 tbsp groundnut oil

4 spring onions, slivered

2 celery stalks, thinly sliced

3 carrots, thinly sliced

100 g/3½ oz baby sweetcorn, halved

175 g/6 oz mushrooms, sliced finely

1 garlic clove, roughly chopped

450 g/1 lb raw prawns, peeled and deveined

1 tsp cornflour

2 tbsp soy sauce

50 ml/2 fl oz chicken stock

225 g/8 oz savoy cabbage, shredded

175 g/6 oz mangetout

cooked rice, to serve

1 Put the wok over a medium heat and add the cashew nuts; toast them until they begin to brown. Remove with a slotted spoon and reserve.

2 Add the oil to the wok and heat. Add the spring onions, celery, carrots and baby sweetcorn and cook, stirring occasionally, over a medium–high heat for 3–4 minutes.

3 Add the mushrooms and cook until they become brown. Mix in the garlic and prawns, stirring until the prawns turn pink.

4 Mix the cornflour smoothly with the soy sauce and chicken stock. Add the liquid to the prawn mixture and stir. Then add the savoy cabbage, mangetout and all but a few of the cashew nuts and cook for 2 minutes.

5 Garnish with the reserved cashew nuts and serve on a bed of freshly cooked rice.

wok-fried jumbo prawns in spicy sauce

SERVES 4

3 tbsp vegetable or groundnut oil

450 g/1 lb raw king prawns, deveined but unpeeled

2 tsp finely chopped fresh ginger

1 tsp finely chopped garlic

1 tbsp chopped spring onion

2 tbsp chilli bean sauce

1 tsp Shaoxing rice wine

1 tsp sugar

½ tsp light soy sauce

1–2 tbsp chicken stock

1 In a preheated wok, heat the oil, then add the prawns and stir-fry over high heat for about 4 minutes.

2 Arrange the prawns on the sides of the wok out of the oil, then add the ginger and garlic and stir until fragrant. Add the spring onion and chilli bean sauce. Stir the prawns into this mixture.

3 Lower the heat slightly and add the Shaoxing, sugar, light soy sauce and a little chicken stock. Cover and cook for a further minute. Serve immediately.

chilli prawns with garlic noodles

SERVES 4

200 g/7 oz cooked king or tiger prawns, peeled and deveined

4 tbsp sweet chilli dipping sauce

4 tbsp groundnut or vegetable oil

4 spring onions, chopped

55 g/2 oz mangetout, trimmed and halved diagonally

1 tbsp Thai red curry paste

400 ml/14 fl oz coconut milk

55 g/2 oz canned bamboo shoots, drained and rinsed

55 g/2 oz fresh beansprouts

115 g/4 oz dried medium egg noodles

2 garlic cloves, crushed

handful of fresh coriander, chopped

1 Toss the prawns with the chilli sauce in a bowl. Cover and set aside.

2 Heat half the oil in a preheated wok, add the spring onions and mangetout and stir-fry over a medium–high heat for 2–3 minutes. Add the curry paste and stir well. Pour in the coconut milk and bring gently to the boil, stirring occasionally. Add the bamboo shoots and beansprouts and cook, stirring, for 1 minute. Stir in the prawns and chilli sauce, reduce the heat and simmer for 1–2 minutes until just heated through.

3 Meanwhile, for the noodles, cook in a saucepan of lightly salted boiling water for 4–5 minutes until just tender. Drain and return to the saucepan.

4 Heat the remaining oil in a small non-stick frying pan, add the garlic and stir-fry over a high heat for 30 seconds. Add to the drained noodles with half the coriander and toss together until well mixed. Transfer the garlic noodles to warmed serving bowls, top with the chilli prawn mixture and serve immediately, garnished with the remaining coriander.

prawns with straw mushrooms

SERVES 4

2 tbsp vegetable or groundnut oil

bunch of spring onions, trimmed and chopped

2 garlic cloves, finely chopped

175 g/6 oz creamed coconut, roughly chopped

2 tbsp Thai red curry paste

450 ml/16 fl oz fish stock

2 tbsp Thai fish sauce

2 tbsp Thai soy sauce

6 sprigs fresh Thai basil

400 g/14 oz canned straw mushrooms, drained

350 g/12 oz large cooked peeled prawns

cooked jasmine rice, to serve

1 Heat the oil in a preheated wok and stir-fry the spring onions and garlic for 2–3 minutes. Add the creamed coconut, red curry paste and stock and heat gently until the coconut has dissolved.

2 Stir in the fish sauce and soy sauce, then add the basil, mushrooms and prawns.

3 Gradually bring to the boil and serve immediately with freshly cooked jasmine rice.

ginger prawns with oyster mushrooms

SERVES 4

3 tbsp vegetable oil

3 carrots, thinly sliced

350 g/12 oz oyster mushrooms, thinly sliced

1 large red pepper, thinly sliced

450g/1 lb large prawns, peeled and deveined

2 garlic cloves, crushed

coriander leaves, to garnish

cooked rice, to serve

sauce

150 ml/5 fl oz chicken stock

2 tsp sesame seeds

3 tsp grated fresh ginger

1 tbsp soy sauce

¼ tsp hot pepper sauce

1 tsp cornflour

1 To make the sauce, stir together the chicken stock, sesame seeds, ginger, soy sauce, hot pepper sauce and cornflour in a small bowl until well blended. Set aside.

2 In a large preheated wok or frying pan, heat 2 tablespoons of the oil. Stir-fry the carrots for 3 minutes, remove from the pan and set aside.

3 Add the remaining oil to the wok and stir-fry the mushrooms for 2 minutes. Remove from the pan and set aside.

4 Add more oil if needed and stir-fry the pepper with the prawns and garlic for 3 minutes until the prawns turn pink and opaque.

5 Stir the sauce again and pour it into the wok. Cook until the mixture bubbles, then return the carrots and mushrooms to the wok. Cover and cook for another 2 minutes longer until heated through. Garnish with coriander leaves and serve over freshly cooked rice.

simple stir-fried scallops

SERVES 4

450 g/1 lb scallops

2 tbsp sesame oil

1 tbsp chopped fresh coriander

1 tbsp chopped flat-leaf parsley

cooked rice noodles, to serve

sauce

2 tbsp lemon juice

2 tbsp soy sauce

1 tbsp honey

1 tbsp minced fresh ginger

1 tbsp Thai fish sauce

1 garlic clove, flattened

1 To make the sauce, combine the lemon juice, soy sauce, honey, ginger, fish sauce and garlic in a bowl and stir well to dissolve the honey. Add the scallops and toss to coat.

2 Heat a wok over the highest heat for 3 minutes. Add the oil and heat for 30 seconds.

3 Add the scallops, with their sauce, and the coriander and parsley to the wok. Stir constantly, cooking for about 3 minutes. Less cooking time is required if the scallops are small.

4 Serve immediately over freshly cooked rice noodles.

spicy scallops with lime & chilli

SERVES 4

16 large scallops

1 tbsp butter

1 tbsp vegetable oil

1 tsp crushed garlic

1 tsp grated fresh ginger

1 bunch of spring onions, finely sliced

finely grated rind of 1 lime

1 small red chilli, deseeded and very finely chopped

3 tbsp lime juice

lime wedges, to serve

cooked rice, to serve

1 Slice each scallop in half horizontally, making two circles from each scallop.

2 Preheat a wok over a medium heat and add the butter and oil.

3 Add the garlic and ginger and stir-fry for 1 minute without browning. Add the spring onions and stir-fry for another minute.

4 Add the scallops and continue stir-frying over a high heat for 4–5 minutes. Stir in the lime rind, chilli and lime juice and cook for another minute.

5 Transfer the scallops to warmed serving plates, then spoon over the pan juices and serve immediately with lime wedges and freshly cooked rice.

scallops in black bean sauce

SERVES 4

2 tbsp vegetable or groundnut oil

1 tsp finely chopped garlic

1 tsp finely chopped fresh ginger

1 tbsp fermented black beans, rinsed and lightly mashed

400 g/14 oz scallops

½ tsp light soy sauce

1 tsp Shaoxing rice wine

1 tsp sugar

3–4 red bird's-eye chillies, finely chopped

1–2 tsp chicken stock

1 tbsp finely chopped spring onion

1 Heat the oil in a preheated wok. Add the garlic and stir, then add the ginger and stir-fry together for about 1 minute until fragrant.

2 Mix in the black beans, add the scallops and stir-fry for 1 minute. Add the light soy sauce, Shaoxing, sugar and chillies.

3 Lower the heat and simmer for 2 minutes, then add the stock. Finally add the spring onion, stir and serve immediately.

clams in black bean sauce

SERVES 4

900 g/2 lb small clams

1 tbsp vegetable or groundnut oil

1 tsp finely chopped fresh ginger

1 tsp finely chopped garlic

1 tbsp fermented black beans, rinsed and roughly chopped

2 tsp Shaoxing rice wine

1 tbsp finely chopped spring onion

1 tsp salt (optional)

1 Start by washing the clams thoroughly, then soak them in clean water until it is time to drain them and toss them in the wok.

2 In a preheated wok, heat the oil and stir-fry the ginger and garlic until fragrant. Add the black beans and cook for 1 minute.

3 Over a high heat, add the clams and Shaoxing and stir-fry for 2 minutes to mix everything together. Cover and cook for about 3 minutes. Discard any clams with broken shells and any that refuse to open when tapped. Add the spring onion and salt, if necessary, and serve immediately.

mussels fried rice

SERVES 4

2 tbsp peanut or corn oil

1 large onion, chopped

1 garlic clove, finely chopped

8 large tomatoes, peeled, seeded and chopped

225 g/8 oz paella or risotto rice

about 850 ml/1½ pints fish stock

450 g/1 lb mussels, scrubbed and debearded

400 g/14 oz frozen mixed seafood, thawed

175 g/6 oz petit pois, cooked

2 tbsp chopped fresh parsley, plus extra to garnish

salt and pepper

1 Heat the oil in a preheated wok or large frying pan. Add the onion and fry until just softened. Add the garlic and half the tomatoes and stir together well. Add the rice and stir-fry for 2–3 minutes before adding half the stock and bringing to the boil. Simmer for 12–15 minutes, adding more stock as necessary.

2 Discard any mussels with broken shells and any that refuse to close when tapped. Add the remaining mussels to the wok with the mixed seafood and petit pois. Season to taste with salt and pepper and cook for a further 3–4 minutes, until hot, the mussels have opened and the liquid has been mostly absorbed. Discard any mussels that remain closed.

3 Stir in the remaining tomatoes and parsley. Taste and adjust the seasoning, adding salt and pepper if needed. Serve immediately, garnished with extra parsley.

stir-fried fresh crab with ginger

SERVES 4

3 tbsp vegetable or groundnut oil

2 large fresh crabs, cleaned, broken into pieces and legs cracked with a cleaver

55 g/2 oz fresh ginger, julienned

100 g/3½ oz spring onions, chopped into 5-cm/ 2-inch lengths

2 tbsp light soy sauce

1 tsp sugar

pinch of white pepper

1 In a preheated wok, heat 2 tablespoons of the oil and cook the crab over high heat for 3–4 minutes. Remove and set aside. Wipe the wok clean.

2 In the clean wok, heat the remaining oil, then add the ginger and stir until fragrant. Add the spring onions, then stir in the crab pieces.

3 Add the light soy sauce, sugar and pepper. Cover and simmer for 1 minute and serve immediately.

VARIATION

Replace the ginger with 3–4 medium to hot fresh chillies, finely chopped, for a more spicy recipe.

4

Vibrant Vegetables & Side Dishes

spicy vegetarian stir-fry

SERVES 4

3 tbsp vegetable oil

½ tsp turmeric

225 g/8 oz potatoes, cut into 1-cm/½-inch cubes

3 shallots, finely chopped

1 bay leaf

½ tsp ground cumin

1 tsp finely grated fresh ginger

¼ tsp chilli powder

4 tomatoes, roughly chopped

300 g/10½ oz spinach (de-stalked), roughly chopped

125 g/4½ oz fresh or frozen peas

1 tbsp lemon juice

salt and pepper

cooked basmati rice, to serve

1 In a preheated wok, heat 2 tablespoons of the oil and add the turmeric and a pinch of salt. Carefully add the potatoes, stirring constantly to coat in the turmeric. Stir-fry for 5 minutes, then remove from the wok and set aside.

2 Heat the remaining tablespoon of oil and stir-fry the shallots for 1–2 minutes. Mix in the bay leaf, cumin, ginger and chilli powder, then add the tomatoes and stir-fry for 2 minutes.

3 Add the spinach, mixing well to combine all the flavours. Cover and simmer for 2–3 minutes. Return the potatoes to the wok and add the peas and lemon juice. Cook for 5 minutes, or until the potatoes are tender.

4 Remove the wok from the heat and discard the bay leaf, then season with salt and pepper. Serve with freshly cooked basmati rice.

oyster mushrooms with peanut chilli sauce

SERVES 4

1 tbsp vegetable or groundnut oil

4 spring onions, finely sliced

1 carrot, cut into thin strips

1 courgette, cut into thin strips

½ head of broccoli, cut into florets

450 g/1 lb oyster mushrooms, thinly sliced

2 tbsp crunchy peanut butter

1 tsp chilli powder, or to taste

3 tbsp water

lime wedges, to serve

cooked rice or noodles, to serve

1 Heat the oil in a preheated wok until almost smoking. Stir-fry the spring onions for 1 minute. Add the carrot and courgette and stir-fry for another minute. Then add the broccoli and cook for 1 more minute.

2 Stir in the mushrooms and cook until they are soft and at least half the liquid they produce has evaporated. Add the peanut butter and stir well. Season with the chilli powder to taste. Finally add the water and cook for 1 more minute.

3 Serve over freshly cooked rice or noodles with wedges of lime.

egg-fried rice

SERVES 4

2 tbsp vegetable or groundnut oil

350 g/12 oz cooked rice, chilled

1 egg, well beaten

1 Heat the oil in a preheated wok and stir-fry the rice for 1 minute, breaking it down as much as possible into individual grains.

2 Quickly add the egg, stirring, so as to coat each piece of rice. Stir until the egg is cooked and the rice, as far as possible, is in single grains. Serve immediately.

hot & sour courgettes

SERVES 4

**2 large courgettes,
thinly sliced**

1 tsp salt

2 tbsp groundnut oil

**1 tsp Szechuan
peppercorns, crushed**

**½ –1 red chilli, deseeded
and sliced into thin strips**

**1 large garlic clove,
thinly sliced**

**½ tsp finely chopped fresh
ginger**

1 tbsp rice vinegar

1 tbsp light soy sauce

2 tsp sugar

**1 spring onion, green part
included, thinly sliced**

**a few drops of sesame oil,
to garnish**

**1 tsp sesame seeds,
to garnish**

1 Put the courgette slices in a large colander and toss with the salt. Cover with a plate and put a weight on top. Leave to drain for 20 minutes. Rinse off the salt and spread out the slices on kitchen paper to dry.

2 Preheat a wok over a high heat and add the groundnut oil. Add the Szechuan peppercorns, chilli, garlic and ginger. Fry for about 20 seconds until the garlic is just beginning to colour.

3 Add the courgette slices and toss in the oil. Add the rice vinegar, soy sauce and sugar, and stir-fry for 2 minutes. Add the spring onion and fry for 30 seconds. Garnish with the sesame oil and seeds, and serve immediately.

sweet & sour vegetables with cashew nuts

SERVES 4

**1 tbsp vegetable or
groundnut oil**

1 tsp chilli oil

2 onions, sliced

2 carrots, thinly sliced

2 courgettes, thinly sliced

**115 g/4 oz head of broccoli,
cut into florets**

**115 g/4 oz white
mushrooms, sliced**

**115 g/4 oz small bok choi,
halved**

**2 tbsp jaggery or soft light
brown sugar**

2 tbsp Thai soy sauce

1 tbsp rice vinegar

55 g/2 oz cashew nuts

1 Heat the oils in a preheated wok and stir-fry the onions for 1–2 minutes until they start to soften.

2 Add the carrots, courgettes and broccoli and stir-fry for 2–3 minutes. Add the mushrooms, bok choi, sugar, soy sauce and rice vinegar and stir-fry for 1–2 minutes.

3 Meanwhile, dry-fry or toast the cashew nuts. Sprinkle the cashews over the vegetables, stir and serve immediately.

mixed vegetables with quick-fried basil

SERVES 4

2 tbsp vegetable or groundnut oil

2 garlic cloves, chopped

1 onion, sliced

115 g/4 oz baby sweetcorn, cut in half diagonally

½ cucumber, peeled, halved, deseeded and sliced

225 g/8 oz canned water chestnuts

55 g/2 oz mangetout, trimmed

115 g/4 oz shiitake mushrooms, halved

1 red pepper, thinly sliced

1 tbsp jaggery or soft light brown sugar

2 tbsp Thai soy sauce

1 tbsp Thai fish sauce

1 tbsp rice vinegar

vegetable or groundnut oil, for cooking basil

8–12 sprigs fresh Thai basil, to garnish

cooked rice, to serve

1 Heat the oil in a preheated wok and stir-fry the garlic and onion for 1–2 minutes. Add the baby sweetcorn, cucumber, water chestnuts, mangetout, mushrooms and red pepper and stir-fry for 2–3 minutes until starting to soften.

2 Add the sugar, soy sauce, fish sauce and vinegar and gradually bring to the boil. Simmer for 1–2 minutes.

3 Meanwhile, heat the oil for the basil in a wok and, when hot, add the basil sprigs. Cook for 20–30 seconds until crisp. Remove with a slotted spoon and drain on kitchen paper.

4 Garnish the vegetable stir-fry with the crispy basil and serve immediately with freshly cooked rice.

julienne vegetable salad

SERVES 4

4 tbsp vegetable or groundnut oil

225 g/8 oz tofu with herbs, cubed

1 red onion, sliced

4 spring onions, cut into 5-cm/2-inch lengths

1 garlic clove, chopped

2 carrots, cut into matchsticks

115 g/4 oz fine French beans, trimmed

1 yellow pepper, cut into strips

115 g/4 oz broccoli, cut into florets

1 large courgette, cut into matchsticks

55 g/2 oz beansprouts

2 tbsp Thai red curry paste

4 tbsp Thai soy sauce

1 tbsp rice wine vinegar

1 tsp palm sugar or soft light brown sugar

a few Thai basil leaves, plus extra to garnish

350 g/12 oz rice vermicelli noodles

1 Heat the oil in a preheated wok or large frying pan and fry the tofu cubes for 3–4 minutes until browned on all sides. Lift out of the oil and drain on kitchen paper.

2 Add the red onion, spring onions, garlic and carrots to the hot oil and fry for 1–2 minutes before adding the rest of the vegetables, except for the beansprouts. Stir-fry for 2–3 minutes. Add the beansprouts, then stir in the curry paste, soy sauce, vinegar, sugar and basil leaves. Cook for 30 seconds.

3 Soak the noodles in boiling water or stock for 2–3 minutes (check the packet instructions), or until tender, and drain well. Arrange the freshly cooked noodles in a warmed bowl.

4 Pile the vegetables over the noodles, and garnish with extra basil, and serve topped with the tofu cubes.

bok choi with red onions & cashew nuts

SERVES 4

2 tbsp groundnut oil

2 red onions, cut into thin wedges

175 g/6 oz red cabbage, thinly shredded

225 g/8 oz bok choi

2 tbsp plum sauce

100 g/3½ oz roasted cashew nuts, to garnish

1 Heat the groundnut oil in a large preheated wok or frying pan until it is really hot. Add the onion wedges to the wok and stir-fry for about 5 minutes, or until the onions are just beginning to brown.

2 Add the red cabbage and stir-fry for a further 5 minutes.

3 Add the bok choi leaves and stir-fry for about 2–3 minutes, or until the leaves have just wilted. Drizzle the plum sauce over the vegetables, toss together until well mixed and heat until the liquid is bubbling.

4 Garnish with the roasted cashew nuts and transfer to warmed serving bowls. Serve immediately.

stir-fried chinese greens

SERVES 4

**1 tbsp vegetable or
groundnut oil**

1 tsp finely chopped garlic

**225 g/8 oz leafy Chinese
leaves, roughly chopped**

½ tsp salt

1 In a preheated wok, heat the oil and stir-fry the garlic until fragrant.

2 Over a high heat, toss in the Chinese leaves and salt and stir-fry for 1 minute maximum. Serve immediately.

classic stir-fried vegetables

SERVES 4

2 tbsp sesame oil

8 spring onions, trimmed and finely chopped

1 garlic clove, crushed

1 tbsp grated fresh ginger

1 head of broccoli, cut into florets

1 orange or yellow pepper, roughly chopped

125 g/4½ oz red cabbage, shredded

125 g/4½ oz baby sweetcorn

175 g/6 oz portobello or large cup mushrooms, thinly sliced

200 g/7 oz fresh beansprouts

250 g/9 oz canned water chestnuts

4 tsp soy sauce

cooked wild rice, to serve

1 Heat the oil in a large preheated wok over a high heat. Stir-fry six of the spring onions, with the garlic and ginger for 30 seconds.

2 Add the broccoli, pepper and red cabbage and stir-fry for 1–2 minutes. Mix in the baby sweetcorn and mushrooms and stir-fry for a further 1–2 minutes.

3 Finally, add the beansprouts and water chestnuts and cook for another 2 minutes. Pour in the soy sauce to taste and stir well.

4 Transfer to warmed dishes and serve immediately over freshly cooked wild rice, and garnish with the remaining spring onions.

stir-fried japanese noodles

SERVES 4

225 g/8 oz Japanese egg noodles

2 tbsp sunflower oil

1 red onion, sliced

1 garlic clove, crushed

500 g/1 lb 2 oz mixed mushrooms such as shiitake, oyster and brown cap

350 g/12 oz bok choi

2 tbsp sweet sherry

6 tbsp soy sauce

4 spring onions, trimmed and sliced, to garnish

1 tbsp sesame seeds, toasted, to garnish

1 Place the noodles in a large bowl, pour over enough boiling water to cover and leave to soak for 10 minutes.

2 Heat the oil in a large preheated wok. Add the red onion and garlic to the wok and stir-fry for 2–3 minutes or until softened. Add the mushrooms to the wok and stir-fry for 5 minutes or until softened. Drain the noodles and add to the wok.

3 Add the bok choi, sweet sherry and soy sauce to the wok and toss to mix well. Stir-fry for 2–3 minutes or until the liquid is just bubbling. Transfer the noodle mixture to warmed serving bowls, garnish with sliced spring onions and toasted sesame seeds and serve immediately.

szechuan mixed vegetables

SERVES 4

2 tbsp chilli oil

4 garlic cloves, crushed

5-cm/2-inch piece grated fresh ginger

250 g/9 oz carrots, cut into thin strips

1 red pepper, cut into thin strips

150 g/5½ oz shiitake mushrooms, sliced

150 g/5½ oz mangetout, halved diagonally

3 tbsp soy sauce

3 tbsp peanut butter

350 g/12 oz beansprouts

cooked rice, to serve

1 Heat the chilli oil in a preheated wok and fry the garlic, ginger and carrots for 3 minutes. Add the pepper and stir-fry for another 2 minutes.

2 Add the mushrooms and mangetout and stir-fry for 1 minute.

3 In a small bowl, mix together the soy sauce and peanut butter until combined.

4 Using a wooden spoon, make a space in the centre of the stir-fried vegetables so that the base of the wok is visible. Pour in the sauce and bring to the boil, stirring all the time until it starts to thicken. Add the beansprouts and toss the vegetables to coat thoroughly with the sauce.

5 Transfer to a warmed serving dish and serve immediately with freshly cooked rice.

stir-fried broccoli

SERVES 4

2 tbsp vegetable oil

2 medium heads of broccoli, cut into florets

1 tsp sesame seeds, toasted, to garnish

sauce

2 tbsp soy sauce

1 tsp cornflour

1 tbsp caster sugar

1 tsp grated fresh ginger

1 garlic clove, crushed

pinch of hot chilli flakes

1 In a large preheated wok, heat the oil until almost smoking. Stir-fry the broccoli for 4–5 minutes.

2 To make the sauce, combine the soy sauce, cornflour, sugar, ginger, garlic and hot chilli flakes in a small bowl. Add the sauce to the broccoli. Cook over a gentle heat, stirring constantly, for 2–3 minutes until the sauce thickens slightly.

3 Transfer to a warmed serving dish, garnish with the sesame seeds and serve immediately.

broccoli & mangetout stir-fry

SERVES 4

2 tbsp vegetable or groundnut oil

dash of sesame oil

1 garlic clove, finely chopped

225 g/8 oz small head of broccoli florets

115 g/4 oz mangetout, trimmed

225 g/8 oz Chinese leaves, chopped into 1-cm/ ½-inch slices

5–6 spring onions, finely chopped

½ tsp salt

2 tbsp light soy sauce

1 tbsp Shaoxing rice wine

1 tsp sesame seeds, lightly toasted, to garnish

1 In a preheated wok, heat the oils, then add the garlic and stir-fry vigorously. Add all the vegetables and salt and stir-fry over high heat, tossing rapidly, for about 3 minutes.

2 Pour in the light soy sauce and Shaoxing and cook for a further 2 minutes. Garnish with the sesame seeds and serve immediately.

cauliflower & bean stir-fry

SERVES 4

1 tbsp vegetable or groundnut oil

1 tbsp chilli oil

1 onion, chopped

2 garlic cloves, chopped

2 tbsp Thai red curry paste

1 small cauliflower, cut into florets

175 g/6 oz runner beans, cut into 7.5-cm/3-inch lengths

150 ml/5 fl oz vegetable stock

2 tbsp Thai soy sauce

50 g/1¾ oz cashew nuts, toasted, to garnish

1 Heat both the oils in a preheated wok and stir-fry the onion and garlic until softened. Add the curry paste and stir-fry for 1–2 minutes.

2 Add the cauliflower and beans and stir-fry for 3–4 minutes, until softened. Pour in the stock and soy sauce and simmer for 1–2 minutes. Serve immediately, garnished with the cashew nuts.

cabbage & walnut stir-fry

SERVES 4

4 tbsp groundnut oil

1 tbsp walnut oil

2 garlic cloves, crushed

350 g/12 oz white cabbage, thinly shredded

350 g/12 oz red cabbage, thinly shredded

8 spring onions, trimmed

225 g/8 oz firm tofu, cubed

2 tbsp lemon juice

100 g/3½ oz walnut halves

2 tsp Dijon mustard

salt and pepper

2 tsp poppy seeds, to garnish

1 Heat the oils in a preheated wok. Add the garlic, cabbages, spring onions and tofu and cook for 5 minutes, stirring.

2 Add the lemon juice, walnuts and mustard to the wok and stir to combine thoroughly.

3 Season the mixture to taste with salt and pepper and cook for a further 5 minutes, or until the cabbage is tender.

4 Transfer the stir-fry to a warmed serving bowl, garnish with poppy seeds and serve immediately.

hot & sour cabbage

SERVES 4

450 g/1 lb firm white cabbage

1 tbsp vegetable or groundnut oil

10 Szechuan peppercorns or more, to taste

3 dried chillies, roughly chopped

½ tsp salt

1 tsp white rice vinegar

dash of sesame oil

pinch of sugar

1 To prepare the cabbage, discard the outer leaves and tough stems. Chop the cabbage into 3-cm/1¼-inch squares, breaking up the chunks. Rinse thoroughly in cold water.

2 In a preheated wok, heat the oil and cook the peppercorns until fragrant. Stir in the chillies. Throw in the cabbage, a little at a time, together with the salt and stir-fry for 2 minutes.

3 Add the vinegar, sesame oil and sugar and cook for a further minute or until the cabbage is tender. Serve immediately.

stir-fried long beans with red pepper

SERVES 4–6

**280 g/10 oz long beans,
cut into 6-cm/2½-inch
lengths**

**1 tbsp vegetable or
groundnut oil**

1 red pepper, slivered

pinch of salt

pinch of sugar

1 Blanch the beans in a large pan of boiling water for 30 seconds. Drain and set aside.

2 In a preheated wok, heat the oil and stir-fry the beans for 1 minute over a high heat. Add the pepper and stir-fry for 1 more minute. Sprinkle the salt and sugar on top and serve immediately.

spicy green beans

SERVES 4

200 g/7 oz green beans, trimmed and cut diagonally into 3–4 pieces

2 tbsp vegetable or groundnut oil

4 dried chillies, cut into 2 or 3 pieces

½ tsp ground Szechuan peppercorns

1 garlic clove, finely sliced

6 thin slices of fresh ginger

2 spring onions, white part only, cut diagonally into thin pieces

pinch of sea salt

1 Blanch the beans in a large pan of boiling water for 30 seconds. Drain and set aside.

2 In a preheated wok, heat 1 tablespoon of the oil. Over a low heat, stir-fry the beans for about 5 minutes or until they are beginning to wrinkle. Remove and set aside.

3 Add the remaining oil and stir-fry the chillies and peppercorns until they are fragrant. Add the garlic, ginger and spring onions and stir-fry until they begin to soften. Add the beans and toss to mix, then add the sea salt and serve immediately.

sweet & sour tofu with vegetables

SERVES 4

2 tbsp vegetable oil

2 garlic cloves, crushed

2 celery stalks, thinly sliced

1 carrot, cut into thin strips

1 green pepper, diced

85 g/3 oz mangetout, cut in half diagonally

8 baby sweetcorn

115 g/4 oz beansprouts

450 g/1 lb firm tofu, rinsed, drained and cut into cubes

sauce

2 tbsp light brown sugar

2 tbsp wine vinegar

225 ml/8 fl oz vegetable stock

1 tsp tomato purée

1 tbsp cornflour

1 Heat the oil in a preheated wok until it is almost smoking. Reduce the heat slightly, add the garlic, celery, carrot, pepper, mangetout and baby sweetcorn and stir-fry for 3–4 minutes.

2 Add the beansprouts and tofu to the wok and cook for 2 minutes, stirring frequently.

3 To make the sauce, mix the sugar, wine vinegar, stock, tomato purée and cornflour, stirring well to mix. Stir into the wok, bring to the boil and cook, stirring constantly, until the sauce thickens. Continue to cook for 1 minute. Serve immediately.

spicy tofu

SERVES 4

**250 g/9 oz firm tofu,
rinsed, drained
thoroughly and cut into
1-cm/½-inch cubes**

4 tbsp groundnut oil

1 tbsp grated fresh ginger

3 garlic cloves, crushed

**4 spring onions,
thinly sliced**

**1 head of broccoli,
cut into florets**

1 carrot, cut into thin strips

**1 yellow pepper,
thinly sliced**

**250 g/9 oz shiitake
mushrooms, thinly sliced**

steamed rice, to serve

marinade

**75 ml/2½ fl oz vegetable
stock**

2 tsp cornflour

2 tbsp soy sauce

1 tbsp caster sugar

pinch of chilli flakes

1 To make the marinade, blend the vegetable stock, cornflour, soy sauce, sugar and chilli flakes together in a large bowl. Add the tofu and toss well to cover in the marinade. Set aside to marinate for 20 minutes.

2 In a large preheated wok, heat 2 tablespoons of the groundnut oil and stir-fry the tofu with its marinade until brown and crispy. Remove from the wok and set aside.

3 Heat the remaining 2 tablespoons of groundnut oil in the wok and stir-fry the ginger, garlic and spring onions for 30 seconds. Add the broccoli, carrot, pepper and mushrooms to the wok and cook for 5–6 minutes. Return the tofu to the wok and stir-fry to reheat. Serve immediately over freshly steamed rice.

aubergine with miso

SERVES 4

groundnut oil, for stir-frying

2 aubergines, cut into wedges

1 red chilli, sliced

2 tbsp sake

4 tbsp mirin

2 tbsp shoyu (Japanese soy sauce)

3 tbsp hatcho miso

2 tbsp water

1 Preheat a wok over a high heat. Add a little oil and heat until very hot. Stir-fry the aubergine, in batches, for 4 minutes, or until browned and cooked through. Add more oil for each batch, if necessary.

2 Return all the aubergine to the wok together with the chilli and stir together. Add the remaining ingredients and toss everything together. Cook, stirring, until the sauce thickens. Serve immediately.

stir-fried butternut squash

SERVES 2

1 butternut squash, weighing about 500 g/1 lb 2 oz

6 large shiitake mushrooms

5 tbsp rapeseed oil

½ tsp white peppercorns, crushed

½ tsp coriander seeds, crushed

2 large garlic cloves, thinly sliced

finely grated zest of ½ lemon

½ tbsp rice vinegar

4 tbsp chicken or vegetable stock

2 good handfuls of baby spinach, stalks removed

sea salt flakes

chopped fresh coriander, to garnish

1 Cut the squash in two between the neck and the rounded part. Remove the skin from each piece. Quarter the rounded part and remove the seeds and fibres. Slice lengthways into thin segments. Slice the neck in half lengthways, then crossways into thin semicircles.

2 Remove and discard the tough stalks from the mushrooms, and thinly slice the caps. Heat a wok over a medium–high heat, then add the oil. Add half the crushed peppercorns and coriander seeds. Stir for a few seconds, then add the squash in small batches. Fry for 5–7 minutes, carefully turning with tongs, until lightly browned and just tender. Sprinkle with sea salt flakes. Using a slotted spoon, transfer to a large sieve set over a bowl.

3 Add the mushrooms to the wok and fry for 4–5 minutes, using some of the oil drained from the squash. Add the garlic and lemon zest, and fry for another minute. Sprinkle with sea salt flakes and the rest of the coriander seeds and peppercorns. Add to the squash.

4 Pour any oil drained from the vegetables into the wok. Stir in the vinegar and stock, and simmer for a few seconds until slightly reduced.

5 Arrange the spinach on warmed serving plates. Pile the vegetables on top, then pour over the juices from the wok. Garnish with coriander and serve immediately.

stir-fried asparagus & oyster mushrooms

SERVES 4

500 g/1 lb 2 oz asparagus, cut into 2.5-cm/1-inch pieces

125 ml/4 fl oz chicken stock

1 tbsp cornflour

1 tbsp water

2 tbsp vegetable oil

250 g/9 oz oyster mushrooms, thinly sliced

pinch of chilli flakes

salt and pepper

1 tbsp chopped fresh parsley, to garnish

1 tsp chopped fresh chives, to garnish

1 Steam the asparagus for 4–6 minutes until tender and set aside. Combine the chicken stock, cornflour and water in a small bowl and set aside.

2 Heat the oil in a large preheated wok or frying pan over a medium heat. Stir-fry the asparagus, mushrooms and chilli flakes for 1–2 minutes. Reduce the heat, add the cornflour mixture and cook, stirring constantly for 2–3 minutes until thick.

3 Remove from the heat. Season to taste, garnish with the parsley and chives and serve immediately.

VARIATION
Replace the oyster mushrooms with any other Chinese mushrooms, such as straw or shiitake.